AF429293

THE
Heart's
Plea for Change

RECLAIMING THE TREASURE OF YOUR DIVINITY
AND
THE FREEDOM TO FOLLOW YOUR HEART

Rev. Douglas Simon Sweet

THE HEARTS PLEA FOR CHANGE: Reclaiming the treasure of your divinity and the freedom to follow your heart
Copyright © 2023 *by* Rev. Douglas Simon Sweet

ALL RIGHTS RESERVED
No part of this book may be reproduced in any form, by photocopying or by electronic or mechanical means, including information storage or retrieval systems, without permission in writing from both the copyright owner and the publisher of this book, except for the minimum words needed for review.

ISBN 979-8-218-16410-2
Imprint Rev Douglas Simon Sweet

Front cover Bursting Heart illustration © Joewarut

Scripture quotations are from the New Revised Standard Version Bible, copyright © 1989 National Council of the Churches of Christ in the United States of America. Used by permission. All rights reserved worldwide.

The author shapes the views expressed in *The Heart's Plea for Change* and does not reflect the ideology of Traditional Catholic teachings or that of educators or entities that influenced the author's spiritual formation.

ACKNOWLEDGMENTS

A special note of appreciation to Senior Editor Paul Thomson, whose involvement in shaping the content exceeded my expectations.

PREFACE

Naming all who paved the road I traveled would be a mountain to climb. However, it is imperative to acknowledge the scope of those integral to God's plan for me. I direct my attention to the priests, religious brothers, and sisters who have led, taught, and supported me through a rigorous educational, formational, and spiritual process. The lion's share of credit goes to them, not excluding mentors, directors, doctors, and professors. Each one has left an imprint on my soul. However, please note that the views expressed in *The Heart's Plea for Change* are shaped by my extended spiritual growth and development and do not reflect the ideology of any educators or entities mentioned above or within the body of this text.

Undeniably, I loved my seminary years and the opportunities that followed for sharing faith with the people of God; that love will always remain.

My full hope for this work resides in seeing it for what it is, not meant to tear down the Church but with a wholehearted desire to rethink *"where we have been"* and *"where we are heading."* From that vantage point, God is not directing me to turn anyone away from the Church. Instead, our Creator points to the need to let go of the past for the sake of the future.

C O N T E N T S

INTRODUCTION

But he said to them, 'I must proclaim the good news of the kingdom of God to the other cities also; for I was sent for this purpose' (Lk 4:43).

Like many growing up Catholic, my experiences weaved in and out of precepts, practices, and judgments that often stifle the life of one's soul. Even when that was not the case, images of God flowing from the ancient ideologies are more than enough to have lasting effects. No doubt, many denominations share similar experiences on some levels, more, or less. As a child, I didn't know better, at least, not until the questions rose to the surface of my mind. Eventually, they will!

The work ahead is not another novel about good ole Catholic guilt. Instead, it opens a new and refreshing path into the soul's purpose. However, to cross that bridge, revisiting a sorrowfully broken history is necessary for exploring the Temple Jesus built. Because of the sensitivity and broad scope of the work, I begin with my story.

At age 34, in September of 1987, I entered St. John's Seminary College, Boston, MA, to earn a Bachelor of Philosophy degree. By June 1994, I had achieved a Bachelor of Sacred Theology and a Master of Divinity degree at St. Mary's Seminary & University,

Baltimore, MD. The following year, I was ordained a Catholic priest.

My zeal, tempered by a tedious academic and formation process, heightened my enthusiasm. Inspiring people to unveil the inner light of God has always been my heart's desire. I wished only to shake the world with God's love as God rocked my world!

I cannot say that I feel God is always by my side. In fact, it's better still to say he is always ahead of me. Although I call God Father, I know he/she is more than Father, and that God is Mother and how much more do we not know? However, Jesus called God Father, and I wished for God to be my Father as a child and have since loved God as Father. I do not see him as a religion but as Father to all. However, not all say yes.

With so much debris between God and us, I ask, how on earth are people supposed to reach him? This work intends to clear the rubble. And guess what? This was God's intention long before it was mine. As I often say, God is always ahead of me!

Expressing the honor to give voice to both the Father and the Son is beyond my words. Humbled in prayer, I tentatively listen while knowing this is an extraordinary claim. I cannot explain God's choosing but only deliver what presses on my heart. I have enjoyed the wisdom of God's voice since late 1986. However, I have been shy about making it public for fear of ridicule and rejection. And although knowing God's love, I was still timid about asking God questions because I had the underlying fear that questioning God was disrespectful. I believed I should know God's meaning and how to respond. However, when gaining the courage to raise questions, there was no turning back.

About one decade following ordination, I was starting to see that my calling was not what I understood it to be at first. Although I could not understand my unrest, I could not be more confident that my calling is from God. Consequently, I was determined to spend more time in prayer and reflection, and soon learned God had another plan. As opposed to revealing more about God's love, I was learning more about God's sorrow. Something of paramount concern is standing between God and people, and I was about to learn the depths of the matter.

Although unsure where to start, I began to delve into prayer, study, and research. Sometime afterward, Jesus called me his messenger. I was not clear what that meant but continued in my quest and remain steadfast to this day. Making this striking claim has taken me decades to bring forward.

Stumbling through my fears about reaching people with a message that's not in sync with my priestly underpinnings has been discomforting. However, like the man who discovers treasure in a field, my joy is hard to contain, and I must share with all who will listen. I wish not to offend the Church or my colleagues in any way. Yet, I cannot deny the extent of treasures overlooked.

Although I continue to write, I struggle with the question how to speak over a shield built on the reasoning of men that has continued to be compiled for over two thousand years? In essence, God's intent for humanity is much bigger than most are led to believe. No matter where you stand with God, the underlying truth can change your life! The Father says it another way:

> I do not lord over my children like a king collecting
> taxes and filling his purses. No! Yet, you approach me
> as though you owe me something, and you are not
> paying up! You do not know my love for you! I am not
> blaming anyone. However, the time now is to wake up
> to the truth of my desire for creation, not my
> displeasure. For centuries humanity has been waiting on

me. While on the contrary, I have been waiting for you to wake up to me!

Hence, that is the intention and the focus of this project!

God reveals God's heart, and at certain intervals, the Father presents himself as "I Am, that I Am." When asking God, why? The Father reveals that he is voicing his authority and respect for creation. From that, I glean God knows both the dark and the light side of the human. And, in the enigma of a single breath, he openly bares his heart to shine on man and woman.

Of course, God is not a force to object, never mind defy willfully. God is All that is. Unbelievably, many contradict the love that holds us together and turn against all that God desires for the creation. From your windows, you can see the damage. Throughout the pages ahead, Jesus refers to such ones as "they," meaning those who do not choose the "light." Some are willful, and others do not see.

I say this not to tout God's truth and authority but as a reminder that as loving as God is, this is not a fairytale but the reality of choosing the light or darkness. Some prefer darkness. For those who do not, God needs your light and there is no better time to learn why!

About the Visions

Part 1 is an overview of events leading up to the visions I experienced. They include some brain teasers while in the seminary and are helpful to convey what eventually led me to the visions.

In the visions of Part 2, the historical narratives of scripture set the tone. Revisiting the ancient backdrop is necessary for understanding the kingdom Jesus proclaimed. Homing-in on two critical events in Church history unfolds the ensuing factors that led to dismantling Jesus' foundation. In effect, they demonstrate "where we have been." Part 3 unearths vital truths buried beneath the tumultuous history to reveal "where we are now."

The segments that follow advance the urgent message that Jesus and the Father deliver for gathering God's children. Illustrating "where we are meant to be," the visions set in motion the Father's desire to awaken the divine-human nature.

By reclaiming the new paradigm Jesus lived and died for, the visions I deliver unfold like a stairway leading into the kingdom Jesus proclaimed. Each one drawing one deeper into divine love. Although ethereal, the steps align with the Father's plan and pave a path to him. Indeed, Jesus built a stairway to heaven though it is up to us to climb.

You are about to undertake a journey into the kingdom. However, to get started, I warn that the visions in Part 2 can be unsettling. The history that weighs on its entrance is lamentable and may weigh heavily on many hearts. Nonetheless, breaking the lock that seals the doorway into the kingdom unveils the tragic truth that keeps it shut. To say so may sound harsh. However, it comes with love, and God intends to make the truth known for the sake of divine love. Hence, the kingdom slowly unfolds when sifting through the misunderstanding of the early centuries of stress and discord.

Before Getting Under Way

It compels me to make a significant point for a deeper understanding of the work ahead. I pause here to highlight the legacy of the great St. Francis of Assisi. Coming from a wealthy family, he sought to exchange clothes with a beggar for testing the direction compelling him. Dressing in the tattered garment, he ventured into the nearby forest, where he confronted a band of marauders. They grilled him, and Francis replied, "I am the Herald of the great King."[1] When finding nothing of value on him, they mauled him and tossed him into a ditch.

Yet, with the unmatched value of God's favor, three times from the crucifix, he heard Christ say to him, "Go Francis and repair my house, which as you see is falling into ruin."[2]

As in my experience and with many who do not readily understand God's wisdom, the Saint went about cleaning the deteriorating Church in which he prayed. He began the restoration by sweeping floors, polishing rails, and repairing stairs and walls. However, God's call was far more intense in purpose, and the great Saint would accomplish it in due time. Working through trial and error, he found his way.

By divine providence, his purpose was to reform the Church. And here, Francis found his way into a unique calling. As history acknowledges, Francis and his followers' radical stance in poverty pulled on the reins of the Church as it was slipping into the grips of wealth and power. Their extreme poverty was the instrument God used to get the attention of Church authorities that eventually led to reform and cemented the legacy of the eternally renowned Saint.

---

[1] Celano, Chapter Titles, Part 1, The first Life of St. Francis, *St. Francis of Assisi, Omnibus of Sources*, Fourth Revised Edition, Edited by Marion A. Habig, Translations by Raphael Brown, Benan Fahy, Placid Hermann, Paul Oligny, Nesta de Robeck, Leo Sherley-Price, Franciscan Press, Quincy University, Quincy, IL 1991 (Chapter VII, pages 241-242).

[2] Englebert, Omer *St. Francis of Assisi: A Biography*, Second English Edition, Translated by Eve Marie Cooper, Revised and augmented by Ignatius Brady O.F.M. and Raphael Brown, Servant Books, Ann Arbor, Michigan, 1979 (Chapter 3, p33).

Indeed, he became the most outstanding herald the world has known apart from the Son of God.

I do not wish at all to compare myself to the great Saint. That is different from my reason for bringing this example forward. First, I only demonstrate the extent of the Churches' derailment and how Christ framed the problem. Second, from his depths, Jesus expressed dire concern for his Church falling to ruin. Third, God's patience and compassion are displayed even in his grief. In and through the Saint, Christ's intent to alter the Churches' course must not go unnoticed.

Without the intention of comparing myself to the magnitude of the great Saint, I turn to an analogy. You know of minor leagues and major leagues in the realm of sports. I do not see myself in the same company as St. Francis, but his spirit washes over me as I pray, and I believe for a good reason. Though I see myself in the same arena, and that arena is no less drawing near to the heart of God who is calling for change because something is not in sync with the Father's intentions.

Unlike the Saint, while wondering if I was too late, I questioned the purpose of my calling. After a long pause, Jesus made it clear to me that "people are stuck." I drew back! Then, folding my arms, my head bowed to the silence seizing my heart. I had no idea how I was to address the problem or know exactly the meaning but that it was serious. Realizing the importance, I continued to write. Sometime afterward, I received the first vision, and a corridor opened to show me the way. Often, I refer to the visions as "the showings."

PART 1

Beneath the Visions

From Fear to Love

Divine Path Not So Divine

In November of 1986, I brought my mother to a Catholic healing service. On that special sunny day near the end of fall, we stepped inside the shadows of the dimly lit Church. Its light filtered through the magnificent stained-glass windows. I would have enjoyed spending time in the sun. However, my mother's condition pressed on my heart. Although she grew weaker, I insisted things would change. I held her close to my side as we gingerly walked step by step toward the front of the Church.

Stories of praise circulated the region concerning the gifts of the acclaimed healer. I felt confident that something big would happen. Diabetes' assault on my mom was disturbing, and on that day, I could hardly conceal the silent hope burning inside me. My mother was an amputee, but that was the least of her problems.

Opening with song and prayer, all gathered in procession toward the sanctuary. The moment he laid hands upon her; she fell swooping to the floor. My heart could not keep from dropping with her. Immediately, I recalled the moments she fell when forgetting she had only one limb. Then fading into sorrow, a piercing outcry unexpectedly snapped me to attention.

The eerie sound of babbling rang in every direction. This was something I have never heard or witnessed. While "slain in the

Spirit" on the sanctuary floor, an older man sat up with tongue involuntarily ejaculating haunting sounds. Indeed, it was discomforting. On a high mission, the priest turned to stop the ritual and asked if there was an interpreter. Adding to the heightened experience, one of his assistants standing far to his left interrupted the query. "Silence!" the priest fired back. But again, she spoke out in defense. Gravely annoyed, his hand rushed to the sky, and like thunder, his voice cracked, "I said silence!"

At the snap of his voice, she fell hammering to the floor with no more grace than a falling rock. I would not have expected my heart could sink any further. Now, I was shaken and bewildered. Following the startling sequence of events, the healer repositioned himself and asked again. The hand of a middle-aged woman went up to announce that she had received the interpretation. And so, she began slowly and deliberately to proclaim, "I paid a great price in the blood of my Son, why do you still persecute me?" The sinking feeling within now turned to ashes. In fear, I questioned myself, "Is it I, Lord?" Peering into the empty eyes of those gathered around me, I then turned to the priest, whose perplexing gaze looked to the floor. With bent elbow and chin in hand, he stood still while shaking his head.

Following a considerable pause, he returned silently to the sanctuary and resumed the ritual. I waited for more, but with no response, not even the smallest insight into the Father's plea. Indeed, something big had happened, yet no one could explain.

A Change in Course

I never forgot the shrinking feeling I experienced at that service. Although we left without a cure, we remained hopeful that our prayers had God's attention. I never told my mother, but I left knowing the Father was calling her home. Eventually, I let go; I had to. The previous year, she spent the holidays in the hospital. I only asked that she would be home for Christmas. On December 30, 1986, she passed away. The following year, I entered the seminary, although still bewildered by the events of that day. The Father's haunting words remained with me like a thorn in my side.

Although shaken by the interpretation I remained certain about my calling to the priesthood. By September of 1987, I was on my way. However, the questions prompted by the healing service lingered. By September 1993, I entered my final year of theological studies.

During that time, one professor of theology introduced our class to a wide range of topics. Excitement filled the room as each student bid for a subject of choice. As for me, before I could decide, the last theme fell on my shoulders. I was challenged to unpack a specific area of study queried by the formidable Belgian Theologian, Edward Schillebeeckx. I would never have thought to entertain the idea of whether Jesus had to die for our sins. I enjoyed the topic when discussing his ideology and the breadth of his query. However, I remained inconclusive, and just like the author, I felt that I had come to a dead end.

Little did I know then how far I would carry the question into the future. Although it was never my intention, my early experiences as a priest were squarely placing me on the road for mounting a concise conclusion. Fifteen years later, I saw that it was no accident that Schillebeeckx's work fell on my lap.

If you are at all like me, you will agree the question is incredibly provocative. It begs for a clear answer, especially to a question entirely awkward in a spiritually torn world built on mores surrounding the cross of Christ. Yes, somewhat sticky, but at the same time, creating a reasonable level of doubt in concern for the true meaning of Jesus' passion, mission, and death.

I question how many people are truly set free by Jesus' cross or still burdened by their sins. It is written that Jesus destroys sin, but what does that mean? When looking out my window, it appears that sin is destroying humanity, and we are all feeling it, and the questions continue.

In a world still looking for answers, my hope is that the query you are about to undertake will expand your ability to address unanswered questions of faith, especially to see more deeply into the yearning and satisfaction of your soul.

On to Priestly Ministry

Feeling a blend of joy and sorrow when engaging the community of believers, my opening years as deacon and priest continued with a good measure of rich experiences. I loved delivering a message imbued with the depth of God's involvement in the lives of others. Inspiring others to unveil the inner light of God has been somehow mysteriously my heart's desire. And now, my zeal is tempered by a tedious educational and formational process. I wished only to shake the world of my congregation just as God's love rocked my world and turned my world inside out. Often, I felt as though I was walking on air. Yet, to my disappointment, my enthusiasm soon began to fade.

The most unfortunate experiences came to me within the context of Spiritual Counseling. As it was, many came to me sharing a deeply seated grievance, whether young, middle-aged, or older. To my dismay, rising to the surface was an underlying fear of God's rejection. The tipping point besieged me through the trembling voice of an older man. He approached me in response to a sermon I gave during a daily Mass.

"Father, I know God loves me, but why don't I feel that he does?" Here, I felt I had no compass. Not less than eighty years of age, he was a faith-filled man whose spiritual aspirations inspired the devotions of his entire family. Hardly a day went by that he missed daily Mass. However, his heart was not at peace. The sound of his voice was drowning in tremors of anguish. Although it was a thorny question, deep inside, I knew he was not alone. I responded that I did not know but that I would spend some time in prayer and offer him my thoughts.

Chasing the Fear

Here, I began the arduous journey of tracing my way back to the underlying problem. Countless others came to me with similar anxieties, and now, I was on a path to discover why. And what could be more debilitating than the fear of God's rejection? Because the tension reveals itself in different ways and on many levels in so many lives, I believe the corridor that opened to me was no coincidence.

Angst-ridden, he was twenty years of age when he stepped into my office. Although unsure about what he wanted, his desire for God was written all over his face. I listened for nearly an hour. Finally, I asked, "What are you afraid of?" Because of the growing concern for God's approval, I was becoming familiar with the bewilderment in his eyes and quite adept at knowing when to speak and where to take the conversation. After talking a bit more, he clearly expressed both his fear and exactly what he wanted. Although his unrest remained, he did not want or need forgiveness. Stifled not by human rejection, but by God's, he sought acceptance and a new start. When departing, already he was a different young man.

Whether in my office, confessional, or pew, people spoke less about their sins and more about their unrest. Unfortunately, I soon learned the fear is due, of course, to guilt and lack of self-approval. But from where does it come? Hence, that one question diminished my zeal for parish ministry. I had to get to the root of it! Why are so many good and faithful people suffering on the level of the soul?

By August of 2005, I stepped away from active parish ministry. Although I loved the community, I could not deny my unrest and the estrangement. I had to know why so many people feel alienated from God. In my heart, I was also set back by the question of God's intention. A judge to fear is not the Father I answered to. I was more depressed than walking on air. Something is wrong, and I could not let it go.

After four years of isolation and journaling, I started to see not just the nature of the problem but its foundations. Overwhelmed by the depth of information pouring over me, I struggled to bring it all together. Nonetheless, I saw that my experiences were not by coincidence or about me. It was then that I started to think God may have a different plan for me.

At the time, I admit that I was bitter. By 2009, I had compiled a manuscript and self-published the conclusions. However, shortly afterward, I had the book removed from printing. I still needed more time.

I struggled with presenting the stormy but true meaning of Jesus' life and death. Should I use biblical context and intellectual arguments that may only create more chatter? And how am I to raise my voice over a two-thousand-year-old shield shaped by the voices of the churches? For years I questioned how to gather my thoughts and often wondered if my counterproductive experiences were for my edification only. However, in June of 2016, I received a vision of a "Dagger." For months afterward, Jesus continued the showings. I could no longer deny my calling to deliver God's message.

Soon after, I received the vision of "The Wheatfield." Although I did not fully understand, believing its meaning would eventually unfold, I put it on a shelf. Before completing the book. I was humbled by its significance.

The vision directs my attention to a new paradigm. Unlike the other revelations, the focus shifts, and the clock turns back to the long corridor where my calling began. And again, I am reminded of the Father's plea, although now to forecast a new beginning.

Vision of the Wheatfield

Standing before the Wheatfield, I turn to a path spreading open before me. Stepping into the entrance, as though a parting of the sea, the wheat stems bend backward to open the way. As I make my approach, a clearing unveils, and there I stand within the center of an open circle. Reaching up to the sunlight, the Holy Eucharist descends into my hands. Like the rays of the sun, its luminous golden light fills the landscape. In that light, Jesus reveals:

> The vision of the Wheatfield points to the time of completion, although even with fulfillment, your mission begins. You are triumphant in as much as you have learned the Father's truth. Indeed, it comes at a great price, but that is the way of the Father. Unhampered at the start and steadfast to the end, you understand the Father's plea. Now, you become the messenger.

Are you calling me to celebrate the Eucharist once again?

Your call is to be the bread of life as with all I call. Lead the way, be not afraid. The road is not paved by princes and scholars, but a road paved by those who know the Father's heart. You understand and walk in that light. There is nothing more for you to do.

The Ground of Our Ancestors

Adam & Eve

Setting the stage for the "Visions" means revisiting two crucial themes running throughout biblical history. They are the problem of sin and the fulfillment of God's promise. At the very least, a quick review of some biblical events helps capture the essence of Jesus' saving actions.

The first event is Adam and Eve's disobedience, which is extremely important because the whole of the Bible hinges on it. The next is the cry of the prophets and a word about Moses and the Exodus. Last is the Christ event, and then some notes about the apostle Paul.

Telling the beautiful garden story over and against Adam and Eve's disobedience sets the foundation for advancing humankind's sinful nature and God's wrath. The Creator who saw the creation as "good" now acts as though it's not so good. In relationship to God, we now have long-lasting and conflicting imprints. In effect, paradise is lost, but more frightening Adam and Eve are rejected harshly. The story illustrates the ground of fear on which our ancestors stood.

The Prophets

The problem of sin continues to echo throughout the Old Testament, most significantly heard in the prophets' cries. The stories are told of humanity's plight in relationship to Almighty God. Hence, the illusive struggle for redemption begins.

Through the lives of many prophets that followed, the biblical saga continued. Whether prophecies to rulers or communities, they delivered unrelenting messages to turn away from sin and evil and turn to God. Throughout the Old Testament pages, the prophetic cry echoes, magnifying the understanding that humanity's turmoil is due to sin. Hence, according to the prophets, the coming Messiah will establish God's kingdom and bring blessings to all nations.

Demonstrating the kingdom, they had hoped for, the long-lasting Davidic dynasty is known for being directly tied to God's promise. However, once again failing to meet expectations, the kingdom is dismantled by human sinfulness, and the ground of fear heightens.

The Exodus

Because no other prophet fought harder and more statuesquely than Moses, his story is significant. Biblical history testifies that God acted through Moses to lead the Israelites out of slavery. Interestingly, at the same time, history is also clear that the Israelites never made it to the Promised Land. I have never felt resolved about the predicament and often wonder what happened. Did God abandon them? Hence, does that explain their reasons for rebelling? Either way, it falls back to the same old thing that humanity's sin kept them out of the land of milk and honey. Or did it?

Moses came down from the mountain with a plan understood as God's plan. We know the covenant is founded on the Ten Commandments. But they were on a long journey, and the expectation was about entry into the Holy Land, and that did not happen!

From the viewpoint of a loving Father, to imagine God letting his people down is unnerving. Could it be that the Father presented them with a blueprint to see that the Promised Land is in their hands? This prospect, coupled with the fact that God was not distant from them but opening the way for them, is incredibly provocative.

The story is a gift and credit to God's trust in the integrity of our free will. I believe there is more to the Promised Land than a physical place and that the "blueprints" were not about commandments. Besides, the idea of a covenant does not relate to commandments.

God knows, and we understand how rules and laws are not iron-clad, especially since they don't always produce the highest good and perhaps are prone to failure. In fact, our God-given free will does not match the notion that God desires robots to obey commands. Is that what you would expect of a spouse, or a covenant forged in love?

We have traditionally understood God's offering as a covenant. Why then, would God define God's love through commandments? The difference resides in the freedom to choose. Which is more meaningful? God does not disregard the integrity of free will! After all we are made in God's image. So why would God make such a sacred agreement based on commandments? It makes no sense unless, of course, God proposed a covenant forged in love and then demonstrated through the commandments that the foundation of their desired Promised Land was in their hands.

It's noteworthy to recall, when asked, Jesus declared, love of God and love of one another are the greatest of all the commandments, and then he added that on these two, all the others follow. These two commandments were at the center of all he taught. He did so in both his words and actions. Jesus' direction is less about the rule of law and more about following the heart's way.

The visions I experienced tell the story of God's desire for humanity and the foundation on which to build. Today, the foundation of the Church is crumbling, and much like our ancestors, people are aware that something is missing.

New Testament / New Ground

Still, in search of a Messiah, the prophets' bewailing lingers in the Old Testament's backdrop. The last page turns, and the New Testament begins. We know who the Savior is, and we can see with all due reverence that he is not a political messiah or seeking a throne. Although Jesus is a Messiah with a kingdom, the answer to how he saves is the centerpiece of this work. Most Christians acknowledge Jesus as the Son of God sent by the Father who suffered and died for our sins. Yet, at a closer look, one may see that his life and death carry far more weight. Many say, "The truth will set you free." Jesus handed down the most precious truth of all. Unfortunately, a grave portion is missing.

Here we face the haunting question: Why are so many good and faithful people caught in the snares of God's disapproval? Here again, God's promise in this work is to open the gates. At the onset of Jesus' ministry, he read from the scroll of Isaiah and declared a time of liberation, not shackles of fear (Lk 4:21). I certainly do not deny that often we are the cause of our pitfalls. And could it be that we created them long ago?

When turning to Jesus' proclamations from the beginning, his focus was not on humanity's sin. Unlike the prophets, he sat with sinners. Instead, he focused on the kingdom of God. His direction was crucial to understanding. We know how difficult for his apostles to comprehend this, and no less for us today.

Even within graduate studies, I once heard a Doctor of Sacred Theology lament this mystery of God's kingdom. Fraught by a hint of despair about Jesus' proclamation, she asked, "Where is this kingdom that Jesus proclaimed that is now but not yet complete?" She nearly shouted, "Is it in the in-breaking of Jesus' miracles? Is it in the miracle of the multiplication of loaves? Or healing of the blind man; where?" Undeniably, she was not asking a rhetorical question but genuinely stressing for an answer.

The anxiety expressed in her questioning never left the depths of my soul. At various junctures, this stumbling block crossed my path only to help me connect the dots. No one questions that Jesus proclaimed the "kingdom of God is at hand." However, for the most part, we have pushed that off to the afterlife. Like a problem unsolved, we have placed Jesus' proclamation on a distant shelf outside of time. Although many will say the churches are the kingdom yet divided and subdivided through time.

So, what is this kingdom that is now and not yet complete? Jesus dropped the first clue when reading in the Synagogue. From the scroll, Jesus read the passage of Isaiah that refers to the Spirit of the lord upon him. As he reads, it becomes evident he is talking about his anointing and the Spirit with him. Jesus was not foreshadowing the future but proclaiming the present moment.

He declared good tidings to the poor. He proclaimed freedom to the oppressed and the blind's healing. "Then he began to say to them, 'Today this scripture has been fulfilled in your hearing'" (Lk 4:21). Jesus was not just reiterating the long-awaited promise.

Instead, Jesus was proclaiming the fulfillment of the Father's promise starting on that day!

The reading ahead is a journey within the context of the visions and messages of Jesus and the Father. More than I ever could, God desires that you should know the truth, not to weigh on you, but to lift you and set your heart free.

Jesus declared that his purpose was to proclaim the "good news" of the kingdom, which was why he was sent (Lk 4: 43). The significance of his words can no longer hide behind the curtains of time. Indeed, the kingdom of God is Jesus' central focus and highlighted in and through the visions. Unmistakably, they are for those "who have ears to hear."

A Word About Paul

Because his theology dominates the New Testament, including a note about the great apostle is essential. First, Paul is neither anointed by Jesus nor has firsthand experience of him. Rather, his conversion happened within the range of three years following Jesus' death. And still, questions hang on hooks begging for answers, especially concerning his self-declaration as a chosen apostle.

Historians discuss Paul's violent rampage against the Christians prior to his confrontation with the Risen Christ. Thrown off his horse and struck blind, Paul's life radically changed. For various reasons, the rude awakening is central to understanding Paul. One might imagine how the encounter made him tremble, not because of what Christ did to him, but how Jesus exposed his actions of betrayal. Stymied by this encounter, Paul had much to regret, mainly that he dragged men, women, and children from their homes. Adding to his turmoil is another factor to consider. For Paul, the encounter with the Risen Christ was apocalyptic, signifying that the end was near.

We have two significant contentions running through Paul's mind and heart. To argue that he had no regret for his assault against the Christians is a hard sell. Second, one must bear in mind that for the ancient mindset, Paul's confrontation with the Risen Christ was apocalyptic. For him, the event foreshadowed that the end was near and carried the weight of looming judgment. Here, one can see the complications when attempting to understand his theology. Adding to Paul's complexity, because of the influence of his Rabbinic foresight, his heightened self-reproach is not in character with the kingdom Jesus proclaimed.

Most likely, motivated to reconcile his injustice against the Christians, he sailed across the Mediterranean Sea, establishing one church after the next to undo what he could not. I am not saying there is no merit in that; there is! However, although he established churches in Jesus' name, that does not mean he founded the wisdom of Jesus' truth. Paul was well-read in Jewish law and tradition, but he did not have firsthand knowledge of Jesus to understand his proclamation of the kingdom. The ground on which Paul stood does not align with the foundation on which Jesus stood. As it was, the apostles labored most of their lives to understand Jesus and to embody his message. Paul did not have the privilege.

Before Paul's conversion, he was a grave threat to the Christians. While studying Paul, the renowned theologian, William Barclay, offers an insight that reaches into the apostle's heart. Pondering Paul's mind against the backdrop of his charge against the Christians, the theologian unveils a glimmering light. He writes,

"Paul had to ask himself what secret these simple people had which made them face peril and suffering and loss serene and unafraid."[3]

One may say such a "secret" exists, although not meant to be a secret. Indeed, the Father and the Son lament its loss and reveal it again within the pages ahead.

Paul (Saul) the Pharisee

In the revelations of Part 2, Jesus carves the way through a torn history, and three irrefutable themes about Paul unravel: His grounding in Judaism, he did not know Jesus, nor the kingdom he proclaimed.

Although Jesus was a Jew, he had issues with many laws and practices. He said, "They weigh them down with heavy burdens, and do nothing to lift them off their shoulders." First, Paul was a Pharisee, understood Jesus' cross through the lens of his Rabbinic education, and carried the burden of his human nature through life. Paul wrote, "I know that nothing good dwells within me, that is, in my flesh. I can will what is right, but I cannot do it" (Rom 7:18). Many scholars agree that Paul presents the law as God's will to reveal humanity's sinful nature. Jesus does not. Jesus focuses on the divine nature of God, man, and woman.

Paul Did Not Know Jesus

---

[3] Barclay, William, *The Acts of the Apostles* Published by the Westminster Press, Philadelphia, PA, 1976 (Acts 9:1-9, p70).

That Paul did not know Jesus may be puzzling, but highly measurable because Jesus and the kingdom of God are inseparable. Yet, Paul has no understanding.

Paul Exhibits No Knowledge of the Kingdom

Jesus proclaimed the kingdom of God was at hand while the apostle Paul placed the kingdom on a shelf somewhere in the afterlife. Jesus did not. Although Paul must have known Jesus was at odds with some laws and practices, he did not understand the fundamental reasons for Jesus' words and actions. Mainly, Paul didn't realize Jesus' approach entirely flowed from his vision of God's kingdom.

These three aspects of Paul are essential to note. Because his letters were written before all other books of the New Testament, including the Gospels, his influence is significant. Scholars agree that Paul's work is the lion's share and precedes all other books of the New Testament. Unfortunately, some of the lesser minds not only confuse the dating of the books but also Paul's strained relationship with the apostles, as well as some who declared he knew Jesus.

I only claim to know some things in full detail. The scope is much broader than mine! However, I have the knowledge and guidance of God's Spirit to unveil the wisdom of Jesus' mission. Paul had little to work from apart from his Judaic underpinnings. Interestingly, many argue he was chosen to deliver what the apostles could not. The conclusions are for you to decide.

I note that the objective of this work is not about disapproving of Paul. Instead, it's purpose is to reclaim the new paradigm that Jesus revealed and was lost to human reasoning and discord during turbulent times.

PART 2

Where We Have Been

Return to the Ground of Fear

The Invocation

On a cloudy gray morning in June 2016, I sat at my desk to write. While invoking the guidance and protection of the Father, Son, and Spirit, I was unsuspecting when the first vision came to me. As though in a chamber where time stood still, I fixed my gaze on the dagger appearing before me. Eerie as it was, overwhelming awe held me to silence; yet, running through my mind, I questioned its meaning. This was only the beginning. I could not have guessed how long these "Visions" would continue, but they persisted for nearly a year.

Laying down a critical foundation, the first sequence of visions unmasks a history of events leading into the dismantling of Jesus' truth. Identifying reference points for understanding the gravity of loss, they reveal essential truths buried by a tumultuous history.

Slaying Jesus' Living Word

The Dagger

Suspended freely in the shadows of darkness, the "dagger" appears. Hauntingly free, stock, and gruesome, its faded black handle gives way to a crude steel blade meant for only one purpose. Hastening the intensity, the knowledge of Jesus came to me. Shrouded in silence, I heard not a sound. The words came to me, like whispers riding on the wind, though distinct and well measured. Jesus revealed:

Lost Treasure

> The dagger signifies the spear that is known to have pierced my heart. I reveal the metaphor to exemplify the blade that killed my truth.
>
> My message was not about laws, precepts, preambles, or concepts that would confuse people. Many are the stories of guilt, shame, and fear that bind my sheep. I did not come to shackle or judge, or to judge and shackle. My truth is misconceived.
>
> Piercing my heart more deeply, the 'dagger' foreshadows my truth's slaying with the slaughter of my

followers. Is that not obvious? Even more apparent is the power and might in which my followers stood; most suffered more than I. The enemy believed that all would wash away without even a trace.

The ramifications of this simple vision left me agape. What gravity of truth collapsed in the aftermath of Jesus' persecution and death? The vision reveals a significant loss with the graves of the martyrs. As it was, his greatest agony is less his cross and far more the persecution and deaths of his followers.

Through this manifestation, Jesus makes a point that is extremely clear concerning a critical understanding that history does not tell. His lost truth is so rich in importance that it hurt him more than the cross we have venerated for over two thousand years. The agony he endures is not resolved. His pain is not only for his followers' deaths but the loss of something for which they all lived and died.

We know the historical event of Christian martyrdom. However, because we do not see the destruction of a precious gift, we are blind to the enemies' victory. A treasure displaced that the Father gives through the life and blood of the Son. At the very least, we do not have the full giving of the Father that Jesus handed down to us.

When unraveling the loss that Jesus brings to the surface, knowing where to begin is not easy. All the same, Paul's pharisaical actions render a good starting point. Only a few short years following Jesus' death, Paul, known as Saul, began a campaign against the newly developing Christian communities. In concert with the Jewish Elders, he relentlessly exercised judgments and arrests, commandeering the way to persecutions and deaths. As history contends, he did so with brute force. Deepening the wounds to the Son, his actions play a significant role in elevating public awareness, disgrace, and prejudice against them. Indeed, Paul did not know that he was setting himself up for a heavy burden to carry.

Apart from Paul, the more severe persecutions were still to come yet another three decades after Jesus' death. In 64 C.E., an enormous fire burned for six days to destroy ten of fourteen Roman districts. Ancient historians blame the infamous Emperor Nero. Whether right or wrong, he attributed blame to the Christians. Igniting a flame of terror against them, it burned into the early part of the fourth century.

Jesus reveals that when the martyrs died, the sacred truth beneath his stories died with them. The "Oral Tradition" may have continued; however, Jesus' treasure did not. To define the purpose of the first segment of visions, Jesus unravels a torn history of events to illustrate the burial grounds of his most significant gift to humankind.

Opposed to scattered sheep, those who followed him were individuals and families who drew near to him. Be sure he knew them by name, and his heart broke at the loss of each one. Following his death, they continued in the strength of faith to claim the living library of Jesus' truth. Unfortunately, things got messy and increasingly complicated.

Apart from their deaths, the martyrs' stories do not accurately convey over time. Who can definitively explain the essence of their faith? We do not know all that the Historic Christ said and did. Knowing the stories is one thing while experiencing them is another. Drawing us closer to divine truth, the martyrs leave us the treasure of their blood to contemplate. What secret lived in them to move them beyond belief? Was it that Jesus' cross was for their sins, or something even bigger? Sadly, we do not have the full view that shaped their hearts, and that is Jesus' more considerable anguish, and it did not end there.

I recall the experience of God's presence. I have no words to accurately define it other than an engagement beyond explanation. I will forever remember how it made me feel as if I was on top of the world. So, it was with many of Jesus' followers. A divine connection between God and humans exists, and Jesus was making the connection. Unfortunately, the most significant points of contact have fallen from the pages of history.

Not many understand today the setback caused to the kingdom of God that Jesus proclaimed. The martyrs' lives open a window from which to see into profound depths. Reaching beyond the realm of reason, adamantly, they did not deny the Risen Christ. Instead, they held their ground to death. Without words or writing, they set into motion a vision that only the heart might comprehend.

Slaughter in Jesus' Name

The Torch

Jesus is showing me a mighty hand raising a blazing torch. Captive to the moment, I anticipate what else might follow. Strapped in a crudely spiked wrist band, mightily, the tyrant shakes the fiery lantern. The barbaric gesture shudders through me, and my soul ever so still, then turning to Jesus, already one step ahead:

Heaven's Dark Night

> The torch, signifying my people's ruin, is much like your modern-day lingo 'burning down the house.' And that is what my adversaries attempted to do by wiping out any trace of my followers. Here, to the point of assaulting anyone who would dare mention my name, let alone pay me homage or see me as a Golden Gate. And do not let anyone fool you, the Torch of Terror burned for another fifteen centuries. Although the Declaration of Religious Toleration in 313 C.E. led to immobilization of the Christian persecutions, the nightmare did not end.

The episode that I reference is one of the heavens' darkest moments. You have the term, 'So on earth, as it is in heaven,' here is a clear illustration of this truth. Indeed, the dark ages on earth so too were in heaven, and I say this not lightly. To be clear, what is below affects what is above. You belong to God, who is above, and God is affected by what happens below. During this terrible period, one grievous event led to another.

To put this into perspective, Jesus turns our attention to the growing apprehension affecting the Christian communities. Within a few decades, the growing tension reveals through the Roman Empire's aggression against the Christians. Their assaults were equivalent to the leveling of the Temple Jesus built. And still, the turmoil did not end there.

We know little about the martyrs when compared to what we know about those who persecuted them. Most think of the Roman Empire and its violence against them that continued for over two centuries. In retrospect, little is said about the apostle Paul and his scourge against them. Nor do we consider the declarations of the Church for the torture and killing of heretics. Yet, Jesus emphatically declares the "Torch of Terror" continued for fifteen centuries.

The frame of reference follows shortly after the Council of Nicaea in 325CE (The first official gathering of the early Church) and closes with the end of the Spanish Inquisition in 1828.[4] (The persecution of Christians surged in Spain in the mid fifteen hundreds and continued into the early part of the nineteenth century). Between

---

[4] Kamen, Henry *The Spanish Inquisition: A Historical Revision,* Fourth Edition, Yale University Press, New Haven & London, 2014.

the many centuries, the obscure history still haunts the halls of heaven. Jesus sets the stage for resurfacing yet another long-forgotten era of oppression and torment, where more grievously the torch burned in God's name.

The first segment of visions may be hard to bear. They were for me, but what weight placed on the divinity to behold centuries of torture and death, some unimaginably heinous? The Father and Jesus intend to be clear about unfolding the events that tragically impacted God's most precious gift. Jesus is clear that understanding what went wrong is necessary for realizing the devastation to the Temple he built.

Concerning the undoing of Jesus' sacred mission, Paul is a significant factor. His aggression against the Christians began only a few years after Jesus' death. While on the other hand, the Roman Empire's assaults began approximately three decades after the fact. Something is to be said about Paul's self-righteous campaign.

Paul's Grounding in Judaism

At that time, Paul, known as Saul, wreaked havoc on the Christian community. He did not halt his path of destruction against them until a miraculous intervention with the Risen Christ. His aggression raises some critical questions that scholars debate to this day.

Some educators say that Paul hated the Christians. However, the controversy continues as to why Paul fiercely campaigned against them. Some say he hated them because the Christians believed in Jesus as Messiah. And, to make it more confusing to some, it makes no sense since Jesus was Jewish. Therefore, they question why Paul would be offended.

Others will argue that is the point of contention, because Jesus spoke out against aspects of the law and traditions. As such, some will argue the case of Paul's contempt for the Christians.

No doubt, Paul became a bold legionnaire for God. He traveled throughout the Mediterranean Sea with exceptional determination, likely exhibiting the same intensity unleashed against the Christians. His platitudes reflect his forcefulness, while other times, he is self-effacing beyond measure. He demonstrated two extremes that he struggled to balance. I am not claiming to be clear about his complexity. Who can know his ancient mindset? Although his words and actions exhibit evidence that he associated God with a strength he struggled to satisfy.

Whether Paul wanted to accept the idea that the Messiah would suffer and die, he could no longer deny it after his encounter with the Risen Christ. It follows that he would perceive Jesus' death through his Rabbinic underpinnings.

Paul's ideology, coupled with our ancestors' failing remedies for sin, adds to his reasoning for defining Jesus' cross as a sacrifice for humanity's undoing. After doing so, Paul developed new definitions for understanding the law's purpose under the spotlight of Jesus' cross. In retrospect, Paul's delivery is complex and confusing, while theologians and scholars continue their debates.

Paul was a Pharisee with staunch views about the sinful nature of men and women. After his conversion, his views influenced the development of elaborate precepts never delivered from Jesus' lips. Jesus came to assist God's people, not to burden them with redefined laws that breed judgment and injury to the soul.

Although Paul does not deny the ineffectiveness of the law to prevail over sin, his perception of Jesus' victory over the law is central to his theological mindset. Consequently, for Paul, the "Good News" is that Jesus frees his people from the insufficiency of the law. Ironically, Paul does not abandon the law but redefines its significance. Most of Paul's teachings are perceived as moral codes and doctrines today. The precepts often confuse and break down the treasure Jesus left in his passing.

Indeed, Paul seeks truth. However, his perceptions are too limited for him to see the bigger picture of Jesus' wisdom. He believed Jesus' cross was the sure answer to humanity's salvation. Whatever the case, Paul's declarations align with our ancestors' perceptions of sin and God's wrath. As it was, the "Doctrine of Original Sin (Rom 5:12-4)" that the early fathers adopted, is not founded on Jesus, but on Paul, who was caught between the throes of God's love and wrath.

Such was not the grounding of the martyrs, let alone Jesus. Regardless of what Paul concluded, he is not the Messiah and did not know him, therefore, to interpret his mission. According to Paul, Jesus' cross was the ultimate sacrifice to deliver us from sin and the law's shortcomings. The question is, was this Jesus' purpose or Paul's interpretation?

Indeed, Paul had a profound experience and earnestly sought to understand Jesus. However, his perception was limited to what he knew through Jewish law and tradition. Although he claimed to be chosen, he did not demonstrate the wisdom of the Messiah. Remember, Paul had no first-hand experience of Jesus.

Paul was sure that Jesus' death was atonement for humanity's sins, and he believed the action of Jesus' cross was far more potent than the law. Indeed, for Paul, Jesus' cross supersedes the law, although attempting still to redefine the law through his ability to understand God's plan. Paul was not wrong to say that Jesus' cross outweighs the law, but "how it does that" is the question in concern for which I write.

Unfortunately, the one essential truth Paul did not know is the meaning of the kingdom of God. Jesus "…said to them, I must proclaim the good news of the kingdom of God to the other cities also; for I was sent for this purpose" (Lk 4:43). The apostles lived and preached the kingdom at Jesus' side. Paul did not. And the apostles were commissioned to do the same, "and he sent them out to proclaim the kingdom of God and to heal" (Lk 9:2). Here too is the vast chasm between Paul and the Twelve.

Consequently, given Paul's propensity to understand the law according to his view of God's will, he extended his reach far beyond the Ten Commandments. Paul struggled with this, and his perspective continues to influence different views and disagreements of today. His reasoning was unlike that of Jesus.

Jesus taught his followers to align with the Father's heart. One may recall that Jesus said the first two commandments are the greatest, and when keeping them, all the others are fulfilled (Mt 22:35-40). They are to love God and one another. Although Paul understood God's love, he did not have the full vision of God's saving love. Judgments do not flow from Jesus' wisdom.

Sometimes Paul speaks as though he is standing on a platform of mores because his delivery results in misinterpretations and judgments.

If anything, Jesus spoke out against judging others. At times Paul's denigration works contrary to Jesus' teachings. Setting such a precedent is contrary to the kingdom that Jesus proclaimed. In retrospect, Paul's work, especially concerning human sexuality, leads people to throw stones.

The apostle's reasoning is complex and often paradoxical, adding to the kingdom of God's division. In particular, the divide exhibits when people question whether salvation is through good works or faith alone. Do we do nothing, or is there anything we can do to grow into the image of God who makes us? Must it be a choice to obey laws, or are we called to walk a higher road? On the other hand, through parable after parable, Jesus delivered uncomplicated paths for spiritual growth and development, and the multitudes followed him.

Although Paul knew Jewish law and tradition, that does not mean he understood Christ's fundamental ground. Quite the contrary! Paul did not know Jesus, nor did he have any books to read about him. Because Paul's perceptions of Jesus derived from his understanding of Jewish law and tradition, he interpreted Jesus' cross as a sacrifice for our sins. On the other hand, Jesus declared that he was sent explicitly to make God's kingdom known. The visions focus on a wider scope for viewing Jesus' saving life as opposed to God sending a sacrificial lamb for our sins.

When reverting to the law, Paul suggested the law is for the unlawful, but for those who believe, that God's love supersedes. Do you see how complicated Paul can be? His ideas leave too much behind and fall short of the wisdom of God as demonstrated in Jesus' teachings. Whatever the contention, Paul demonstrated no knowledge of the kingdom Jesus proclaims. The point is a paramount consideration because the kingdom of God was Jesus' proclamation from day one and the holy ground for the "Good News."

The ground on which the apostle Paul stands is like our ancestors,' who feared a wrathful God. Jesus is portrayed as the Sacrificial Lamb who ironically saves us from the very Creator who made us. His portrayal of God is not much different than our ancestors, only with a different twist. In this case, the precept implies we should fear God. Hence, the defining line between Paul's assertions and Jesus' teachings, and the implications are monumental.

Jesus' proclamation hinges on God's kingdom. A ground, unveiling throughout Jesus' entire life and unfolding within each vision. When Jesus lands the phrase "burning down the house," he reveals the true home of the Father. By ravaging his people, they were burning down the Temple Jesus had built, not of brick and mortar but through the awakening Spirit of the Father within the human heart. Those martyred were living in the joy of the Father's Spirit despite the hardships imposed on them. Etchings on the walls of the catacombs give witness to their songs.

Indeed, through their deaths, persecutors caused the historical destruction of God's living Church that was meant to be handed down from one generation to the next. Today, we lack the full realization of the Temple Jesus constructed, which is better understood when Jesus vowed to build the Temple in three days.

The Temple of the Elders in Jerusalem drowned out joy and celebration with its precepts and practices weighing heavily on people. The weight continues today and often manifests through the symptoms of a broken soul. Instead of celebrating the joy of life in the Father, many live in fear of their unworthiness. At the least, the numbers are high when counting those living in uncertainty.

Today, precepts and practices invalidate not merely the actions of those in question but who they "are" at heart. As such, the strike is straight to the soul. In retrospect, the Spirit within them shrinks. Such was the case of the man who asked me, "I know God loves me, but why don't I feel that he does?" Although confessing his sins, the man saw himself unworthy because forgiveness does not necessarily mean God's acceptance, especially when repeating scenarios of sin and forgiveness that are short-lived. Consequently, one continues to feel like a sinner. This is a grave offense to the soul's life.

When Jesus portrayed himself as the "Golden Gate," he does so in as much as he shows the way to the Father. He did not open the gates of heaven. He opened humanity's eyes to the gateway of the Father's heart that never closed. Given the lack of understanding following the destruction of his followers, Jesus' truth was buried with them. When Jesus said he could rebuild his Temple in three days, he revealed the Temple that lives in the hearts of those who followed him. Hence, this reveals the adversaries' success in bringing down the Temple he built in the Father's name.

Harvesting Jesus' Written Word

The Sickle

The vision of a sickle opens to me, conveying the forceful energy for plucking and pruning. Shaved to a point, its crescent shape and sharp edge are chilling. Jesus reveals:

Harvesting the Written Word

> The 'sickle' represents the harvesting of my truth, but not reaping the truth to feed my people, rather to keep it from my people. And they did so by taking my precepts and finding antidotes to quell my truth. It was a means of cutting away my truth and derailing it. An example of this unfolds from a story which every Christian is familiar.
>
> If you are reading this, then chances are you have heard the story of the 'Adulteress Woman.' I did not dismiss her by telling her to 'go and sin no more.' Instead, that is the derailment. It was quite easy when one thinks of it. And the truth is, I told her to go away from here, be not afraid. Know that you are loved and that I do not condemn you. And people, when they hear

these words, it will not be new to them because this truth
is embedded deep within them.

I do not pretend to know the depth of history beneath this vision,
at least not in every detail. However, I am clear about Jesus'
message. We may have ideas about when, how, who, and what
biblical writings were compiled or written, but the details are mostly
hidden in ancient history. However, what is uncontested rests on the
shoulders of the apostle Paul and his theology. His writings predate
the New Testament scriptures, except perhaps the Book of James.
Scholars still debate the dating.

Beloved Jesus, the agreement among scholars concurs with my
observations. However, others confuse the dates, and sometimes the
who, and what; how do you reconcile them? Jesus answers:

> To reconcile is not an issue of knowing every date and
> player, but a matter of my word. My truth was dispelled
> with my followers' deaths and replaced with the
> ideology of the apostle Paul. You have unveiled most
> proportionately and accurately the differences. History
> supports your findings, needless of the conclusions of
> those who guess at the records.

I ask you then: Because so much was at stake, why was Paul
allowed to take things as far as he did?

> Indeed, Paul was not in step with my teachings but did
> not realize it. To hurt him was not in the interest of the
> greater good, but to convert him. Although he did not
> adopt my truth, he made a significant turn in the
> direction toward a higher truth. However, he developed

his reasoning through the education he knew. Here is why he believes himself the chosen apostle. He felt as assured as you, dear writer, about his call to get the word out there. However, his logic was not part of my plan.

Free will is unpredictable, which is why it is an esteemed gift because, in the wisdom of the Father, free will is an avenue for humanity's growth and acknowledgment of God. Most do not understand the potential for being at one with the Father while in the flesh. As you can see, for Paul, the idea is futile. Yet, I, the Son, proclaimed to be at one with the Father.

Take note that I called those who followed me, brothers, and sisters. I did not claim them as adopted but as true sons and daughters of God. Ironically, even Paul experienced the presence of the Holy Spirit. Yet, as you know, his interpretation comes through the lens of his old underpinnings. Consequently, he cannot grasp the meaning of the kingdom I spoke of. Nevertheless, that was not his cause. Instead, to be redeemed from his perceived state of hopelessness.

Hence, as Messiah, I was his hope for redemption and reasons why he still clamored about his fallen nature instead of realizing the full blessings within his soul. He never fully embraced the gift of himself, which is not my intention or the Father's. Creation is a gift, and humanity stands at the center. I conveyed this truth to my followers that they may intimately relate to the image of God by which they are made.

Because you compare my conviction to that of Paul, what makes me different than Paul?

You know already the difference. I say so, only for those
who do not. You have entered the kingdom of God. Paul
did not pass through the gate.

I do not discredit Paul's earnest zeal for God and to do right by
God. However, that does not mean he had a full understanding of
Jesus' truth. If he had, then why the continued friction with the
apostles? The issue is especially noteworthy given the relationship
between Paul and Barnabas. Together, they journeyed to evangelize
and establish churches. Eventually, even Barnabas walked away
from Paul.

A significant link was missing, and that link was Jesus'
fundamental mission to establish the kingdom of God. Scholars will
admit that Paul says little to nothing about the kingdom, and in
retrospect, he pushes it off to the afterlife. Jesus did not. Jesus says,
"... the kingdom of God is at hand!"

Nor did Jesus see sin as the overarching obstacle. Instead, he
saw judging others as divisive because it breeds misunderstanding
and fear of God.

Paul sweltered in the problem of sin, which intensified
following his encounter with the Risen Christ. Although struck
blind, he could now see his grave offense against God. However,
through his traditional underpinnings, Paul defines Jesus' cross as
the atonement for our sins. On the other hand, Jesus points to the
kingdom of God with us now; that is our liberation. The void
between them is notable. And here again, recall the proclamation of
Jesus' reading in the Synagogue.

I often wonder why the apostles struggled to understand Jesus,
and then Paul appeared to run with the ball by applying his rabbinic
underpinnings to Jesus' cross. Unbeknown to Paul, he replaced

Jesus' mission with his theology. As Jesus proceeds to unveil the kingdom's full breadth via the visions, one's eyes open, and the differences are tangible.

I do not say that Paul intentionally errs in another direction. Instead, by the nature of his strong character, he was convinced Jesus' cross was the fulfillment of our ancestors' dilemma with sin. And no one could tell him differently. As such, to note that Paul's letters cast a shadow on the developing texts of the New Testament is critical. I am not saying Jesus is any less the Messiah. Instead, his purpose is far more than atonement for our sins!

In this vision, Jesus points to the gathering of the written works, although not to his benefit, whether intentional or not. Consequently, Paul's work influences theological mindsets and, therefore, the scriptures that followed. Henceforth, the emphasis on humanity's sins continues to reverberate throughout the New Testament, only now with a different spin. Jesus' focus was the kingdom of God at hand, and still, not many are aware and believe the kingdom is a place in heaven.

It's interesting to note how history illustrates how far we have drifted from the kingdom Jesus proclaimed. By the seventeenth century, the struggle to define the complicated relationship between the Church and state as the manifestation of God's kingdom came to a head. The question of authority was central to the issue.[5] By the nineteenth century, the relationship between Church and state continued to dissolve.

---

[5] Hobbes, Thomas, *Leviathan*, Penguin Random House, UK, 1651.

Today, countless people refer to the churches as the expression of God's kingdom. Indeed, they can, and some do. However, more is to consider and enough hurt prevailing to reclaim the all-embracing paradigm Jesus intended.

Following the passing of Jesus and the apostles, the community of believers handed down the stories. Eventually, they were put into writing and attributed to the apostles by name. The scope of this is far-reaching throughout the whole of the scriptures. Scholars agree to the many hands over long periods that influenced the writing. No one can say precisely how, when, or where. Yet, we know how easily stories change as they orally pass down the line. However it was, Jesus emphatically declares that his truth was not recorded accurately. To that point, Jesus adds that the writings were gathered and not for the highest and best good. Asking about the details in prayer, Jesus responds:

> If you take the scriptures literally, it can be hard to find me. Those who followed me handed down stories that gave witness to what they never experienced before in a man. My words were not about sin or human weakness, but about God's love for them. And that was the seed for developing their courage to live and to die in my name.

When talking about "harvesting" your truth, and for the wrong reason, I question whether you mean deliberately, or just that what they maintained was not right.

> It was not right, and when questions surfaced, the defense became more deliberate.

Theoretically, Jesus is saying that those writing the scriptures were not deliberately doing so to derail his truth. Instead, they did not have the full measure of Jesus' wisdom, although believing they maintained what was accurate. In effect, their posture continued to grow stronger over the test of time. To a large extent, critical historical research identifies many who wrote in the names of biblical figures. In retrospect, the authors are anonymous. Of course, this is only a peek into a long history of stories and writings passing through many hands.

To underscore the point, the "Letters of Paul" are a good example. Those referred to as the "Pauline Letters" are seven attributed to Paul, while the other six are more likely not by Paul's hand. Such mingling with authorship is not uncommon throughout the expansion of the biblical text. You can see then the challenges that may arise when interpreting the scriptures.

For those interested, my references are based strictly on the Pauline texts. Jesus, I must raise the question again from another angle: Were derailments of your truth incidental due to Paul's influence, or deliberately intended?

> It was a combination of both, but remember, any inferences occurred over time. What became deliberate adhered to the reasoning of Paul. Hence, reasons for disputes at the First Council.

As most are led to believe, are you saying the disputes did not involve heresies only?

> No, they had differences on various levels to the point that Paul's views conflicted, but not against the

majority. As I said, the voice of my truth died with the martyrs.

Am I hearing that the martyr's truth was lost to Paul's reasoning at the First Council?

In theory, it did. However, by that time, no one could distinguish between my truth and that of Paul's. So indeed, questions lingered, but my truth did not.

Jesus and the Adulteress

We turn again to Jesus' use of the "Adulteress Woman" drama to exemplify how collecting stories and melding them with a specific theological influence played out. This narrative demonstrated our ancestors' fear-based perceptions of God and sin. Naturally, they are inclined to safeguard the cross that saves them. However, it does not mean they understood Jesus' saving actions and most certainly the kingdom Jesus proclaimed. The example of the woman caught in adultery is telling given the subtle yet practical nature of the discrepancy.

Many would agree this is the most widely spread story of the Gospels. Profiling the extraordinary wisdom and compassion of Jesus, the story is beautifully rich. Although more profound than what we have been led to believe.

No one can argue the depth of compassion Jesus exemplifies. Interestingly, Jesus uses the vision of the "Sickle" to showcase this story. No doubt, Jesus chose this image for a reason. Here, because in this heartwarming story, a discrepancy points to a break from Jesus' overarching truth.

Although subtle, the effects are hurtful to God's truth because the ground for understanding derails the fundamental purpose of Jesus' mission. In this depiction, we subtly stumble into the weight of law and sin. Yet, Jesus exercised a different approach. He proclaimed, "…the kingdom of God is at hand." He did not come to judge sinners. He came to free them from their oppressors.

What happened in this passage is monumental! He saved her from persecution and death. He demonstrated love for her. He freed her from humanity's condemnation, but then he said to her, "Go and sin no more." Was this Jesus' mandate? Do you feel the weight of this imperative? Many can argue in opposition, but from what angle?

Jesus' words and deeds declare that God is a loving Father, and of course, the Father wills that we do not bring harm to anyone. However, the Father does not get us into that place by pushing us into it by threat or fear. He gets us to that place by loving us into it; that is the light that motivates us! As subtle as the discrepancy may be, it becomes a danger because it confuses God's love with God's judgment. If this woman failed to meet Jesus' mandate, would she not feel the weight of fear?

The sickle signifies a problem that casts a shadow on the nature of God. Unfortunately, we have adapted and lived with it for over two thousand years. I have seen the results and have firsthand experiences of the fallout that has led me to this work. Although subtle, the passage's effects are like cracks in a wall that eventually will fall apart. If the foundation were of Jesus' making, I would not be able to make that statement.

Jesus' approach was far more than a gratuitous act to give her another chance to go ahead and sin no more. Jesus' action surpasses what we are led to believe. His action was one of complete love intended to lift her to freely pick herself up and walk with dignity and without judgment. Is the woman more apt to walk away and sin no more given the condition placed on her? Or will she freely walk away motivated by the love and forgiveness that raises her?

The mandate fits the portrayal of Jesus' character as Lord over sin and judgment. In retrospect, he alone has the power to forgive sins. A pattern is evident that innuendos related to sin, such as "...go and sin no more," are insertions that must flow from Jesus' lips. Authors of scripture deny what the apostles struggled to learn, and Paul never grasped.

For Jesus, sin is not the problem; love is the issue. Judgment on any level does not heal the soul. Love is the antidote, and it can be much harder to deliver, and Jesus showed the way. His mission was to open the path in the name of God's love. He never expressed the way through words of judgment or pointing fingers at the dark side of the human. Instead, he pointed to God's love that draws us into the light of a higher paradigm.

According to Jesus' "vision of the sickle," defining his authority over sin is a product of the scriptural narratives of old. Jesus' authority is of a much higher lifegiving accord! To this day, many weigh in on the traditional definitions of sin, and the saga continues. Jesus intends not to be Lord over sin but that he loves as God loves.

Let's pause for a moment to recall the experience of my first confession around the age of seven. I went into the act wholeheartedly with attention to the prayers. However, the approach backfired. I intended to make a good first confession, and the prayers were more significant to me to do that. However, because the number of times I confessed to a fault did not bode well with the confessor, I was scolded and with the added threat that I was not ready to receive my first holy communion. He was right! I did not spend my time in the futility of counting my sins. Instead, my time was spent learning the prayers.

How could I recall all the times I lied or offended another? After all, seven years is a long time to keep track. How scary to think that God is keeping the records, especially in numbers I cannot recall? Does this have anything to do with Jesus' plan to set us free? I do not say this in anger or to justify my posture, but to make a clear point about the differing viewpoint of Jesus and the Church that set sail after him.

Jesus' action is a call to love as he has shown love. That is the way of the kingdom Jesus proclaims. His focus is on the light of the Father's love, not the problem of sin – instead, focusing on the Father's love; the one true way out of the darkness. As written in the scriptures, Jesus says, "This is my commandment, that you love one another as I have loved you" (Jn 15:12).

During Jesus' trial and persecution, his accusers ridiculed him, spat at him, and handed him over to scourging. Yet, while hanging from his cross, Jesus did not condemn them. He said, "Father, forgive them; for they do not know what they are doing" (Lk 23:34). In contrast, other scriptural passages profess words flowing from Jesus' mouth that suggest the Father's wrath, particularly against his enemies. The inconsistency reflects the nature of humans and gets confusing, and why Jesus said, "... reading literally makes it hard to find me."

Many do not dare question such passages but work their way through them intellectually. And when they do, they are often tied up in knots riddled with complexity. And like a plane flying in circles, they do not see past the static notion of Jesus, Lord, over sins.

At this point, I turn to a reputable source for diving a bit deeper into the matter of the "Adulteress Woman." Scholars believe that within the "Oral Tradition," the story circulated sometime during the second century. Subsequently, researchers identified three different versions of the same story and the narrative written by the fourth century. Interestingly, when the Revised Standard Version of the Bible was printed in (1952), the story was excluded. Who knows why? However, due to protests, the story was retrieved and inserted at the next printing.[6]

Removal at the late date raises questions about those discerning the written word. What was it that compelled them to dismiss the story altogether? At the least, evidence suggests underlying issues or unresolved conflicts of interest. No matter, Jesus is revealing a discrepancy.

In this case, when Jesus said to the Adulteress Woman, "...go and sin no more," most agree that the biblical narrative correctly identified Jesus as lord over sin and judgment. In retrospect, he alone has the power to forgive sins. The conclusions are based on what the researchers have in writing. Unfortunately, Jesus contends the writing comes with a problem that compromises his truth.

Of course, Jesus is lord over sin, not by the force of fear but by the power of love. Love is the strength he gives, not a single iota of anything less. We fear enough ourselves. Why would he replace her burden with another when he declares his "...yoke is easy?" I have witnessed countless good people carrying heavy loads. Again, I raise the question, why?

Paul makes many high claims concerning Jesus' cross and the "Good News" that Jesus saves us from our sins. He speaks with

---

[6] Comfort, Philip W, and Wendell C. Hawley, *Opening the Gospel of John*, Tyndale House Publishers, Inc. Wheaton, Illinois, 1994. (Appendix, *The Woman Caught in Adultery* pages 343-6).

authority, yet he was not chosen by Jesus, of all things, to interpret the breadth of his mission.

Paul Dishonors Peter at Antioch

While I want to discuss a noteworthy incident concerning Peter and Paul in this section, I will first highlight the character of Peter before delving into an occasion at Antioch where Jews and the Gentiles often gathered. We know how important Peter is to Jesus and how his zeal reflects extraordinary love for Jesus and his teachings. Most importantly, although Peter struggled to understand, he never gave up on his love for Jesus. Instead, we see him as the successor, and his wisdom seasoned after the years and tears spent with Jesus.

While attending a gathering in Antioch, no consensus reveals what led to Paul's divisive words against Peter. Galatians 2 demonstrates the underlying tension concerning the question of circumcision. In short, if the Christians of Jewish descent require the Gentiles to be circumcised, then they are subjecting them to Jewish law which was never Jesus' intent. However, some had differing opinions, namely the Judaizers who adhered to the necessity for circumcision. Hence, the tension posed at the meeting.

No one knows for sure what got into Paul's head. Scholars who delve into the history of events surrounding the gatherings suspect the existing tension between Paul and those who differed. Hence, because Peter may not have acted according to Paul's determination, he released his discontent with Peter.

Here is where it gets vague. According to Paul, when the Judaizers arrived, Peter stepped away from the Gentiles when Paul expected him to stand up for them. Hence, he accused Peter of hypocrisy and not standing upright in faith. Because we only have

Paul's disturbing view of the matter, who is to know the whole story?

As it was, Peter sat with the Gentiles in good faith, and he disagreed with the Judaizers (Acts 11:1-10). Was it unlike Paul's nature to exercise intimidation as a remedy for resolving a disagreement? While on the other hand, Peter did not resort to the same tools. Instead, would it not be more like him to arrive at the point of "…shaking the dust off his heels"?

Consequently, Peter left, and Barnabas followed shortly afterward. That anyone believing in Jesus would side with Paul over his chosen Twelve is hard for me to understand. Yet, to this day, both Peter and Barnabas are often condemned because of Paul's accusations. And for Jesus, judgment was not on the table and hardly the work of the kingdom. One must question the legitimacy of Paul's accusations. And as early as the fourth century, an astute theologian of the Church offered forewarning.

I prioritize this moment in Antioch due to a letter written by St. Augustine in 397 C.E. He wrote a letter to St. Jerome, an early father of the Church. St. Jerome became a master of Latin, Greek, and Hebrew and later transcribed the biblical text in the standard dialect of his time. The ancient version is known as the Vulgate. After reviewing Jerome's transcription of (Gal 2:14), St. Augustine wrote to inform Jerome about his cause for concern.

Going straight to the point, he announced that Paul was not telling the truth about Peter and Barnabas. Augustine cites Paul for two matters. First, Paul makes a false claim about Peter and Barnabas when he states they are not acting upright in faith. Second, Augustine keenly notes that Paul's motives are not in keeping with the integrity of the scriptures.[7]

---

[7] Augustine, St. *Letters of Saint Augustine, Classic*, Translated by Rev. J.G. Cunningham, *From Nicene and Post-Nicene Fathers*, First Series, Vol. 1. Edited

In addition, Augustine cites Paul's words that "...before God, I lie not" (Gal 1:20). He compares Paul's declaration with his false accusations about Barnabas and Peter not being faithful to Jesus' truth (Gal 2:14). Then finalizing his plea to Jerome, Augustine adds that if Paul writes what is false about Peter and Barnabas, how can we know what Paul says is true. Not stopping there, he continues with his objections concerning how serious they are. Then, in closing, Augustine kindly urged Jerome to do what he must to rectify the matter.

As I understand it, the letter never reached Jerome. However, that is not the point. It's staggering that, early in history, a renowned theologian raised a red flag concerning the deliberations of Paul. Here is what I would say about Paul's teachings, "I am learning the question is not necessarily about the inspiration, but where and when God's truth begins and ends."

Earlier, I noted the character of Peter, and now we can see the traits of Paul, whose rebuke of Peter at Antioch is chilling. I have not heard commentators question Paul's self-righteous attitude, void of Jesus' wisdom. Augustine declares he is "lying." While Jesus says by your love for one another, others will know you are my disciples. Furthermore, Jesus rebuked those who condemn. Paul's lack of chosen character shines in this event, but the glow is cast on a bleak stage, and some use it to denounce Jesus' beloved apostles and elevate Paul's superiority.

The apostles may not have had writing skills comparable to Paul. Nevertheless, they witnessed Jesus' truth and came to a point of not questioning him. And more importantly, they came to believe in themselves and their intimacy with the Father. Such awareness

---

by Philip Schaff, 1886., Abbreviated Edition by Leinenweber, Kindle Edition, Reed Business Information, Inc, 1992 (Chapter 3, Letter 40, 397 CE).

means more to God than their reading and writing skills. Quite frankly, the learned men were more resistant and created excessive unrest for Jesus and his followers. Because of their ways anchored in law and reason, they had no ears to hear his truth.

Jesus was decisive about choosing his followers. Be sure; the apostles were savvier than many who interpret from the scriptures. Much emphasis is placed on their lack of faith and understanding. Even the messages within this book may display why. We are all faced with a challenge. Not all rests on Jesus' Cross. What would that mean to God? Jesus showed us the way, it's up to us to pick up our mats and walk. The question is about how we are doing that.

As for Paul, he was schooled by the most prominent Elder of his time. Because of his advanced knowledge of the scriptures and Judaic Tradition, it was through this lens that he perceived Jesus as Messiah. Because they believed that sin is at the crux of God's bidding, Paul thought he knew better than the apostles when defining Jesus' mission. Hence, most likely the cause of the disparity between the apostles and Paul.

Although Barnabas tried to make things work with Paul, eventually, even he left him. In the end, Paul's letters overshadowed the work of the apostles and, therefore, affected the overarching truth of Jesus' mission. Again, Jesus sat with sinners. He did not judge them, nor did he see them as sinners. He saw them as God's children. Here is something Paul could not fully imagine, never mind embrace. And let us not forget Jesus' lament over his lost truth with the demise of his martyrs. No question, Paul was also a martyr, but that does not mean he fully conceived the wisdom of the Son.

With Paul, Jesus' truth is less a new paradigm and more of a plummeting to the ground with the Adam and Eve scenario before the written word made its way into the churches.

Although Jesus' mission meant a clean break from the ground of our ancestors under the law, Paul's work does not. In effect, many of the underlying fears endure. Without understanding the meaning of God's kingdom, even scholars are puzzled by questions that linger. Perhaps that is because the ground on which Jesus built is unlike anything that preceded him. And from that foundation, the visions help reclaim the treasury of Jesus' truth.

The Last Supper

Many discrepancies hide within the biblical narratives. To cite at least two other examples may be helpful. The story surrounding the "Last Supper" is central to the point. Paul defined Jesus' cross as a sacrifice for our sins and then spoke of the cup of Jesus' blood as the new covenant. On this precept, the foundation of the Church is cast. Here, Paul associated the cup of Jesus' blood with the forgiveness of sins.

The premise has merit. However, it does not contain the full measure of Jesus' saving action. While an active priest, this eventually became difficult for me. God's love is the light that raises me; yet I felt bound to reminders of sin and forgiveness like reigns holding me away from God's love and acceptance. I wondered about the bearing on those who gathered and with nowhere else to turn. At the time, I did not know how to reconcile God's love with these reminders of sin.

Adding to my unrest, once during the most sacred moment at the altar, I had the uncanny feeling of dirt beneath the carpet on which I stood. As I unravel history, I see what was being revealed to me and why many feel unaccepted, unworthy, and lacking self-assurance. Yet, Jesus' closest followers stood fearlessly before lions. They did so because of their self-assurances in God's love and safekeeping.

Without a doubt, the understanding that Jesus died for our sins fosters a love for him but denies the kingdom he proclaimed, which drafts a much bigger picture not only of God's love but the Father's plan.

I recall asking my congregation, "How many see themselves as spiritual?" Not one hand went up! Why is that? The scenario is the basis for the Father's plea through speaking in tongues, "Why do you still persecute me I paid a great price in the blood of my Son." This plea signals that something is standing between people and God's love and acceptance. The lack of self-assurance denies the true sacrifice of his Son and the giving of God held away.

Jesus, at this point, I turn to you to ask: Am I wrong to say that when giving the cup of your life and blood, you intended to release the wellspring of the Father's love for the life of the world?

> I told my disciples to take and eat. This is my last meal with you. Remember me. I am the life of the world. Be bread as I am bread for the life of the world. Drink of my cup to remember, the Father and I are one with you.

Extraordinary! I am forever your priest.

I do not deny the sacred truth of the Eucharist and the miracles attesting to the blood of Christ. However, they are not for bolstering the precepts of the Church but for revealing God's heart. What is more in keeping with the Father than the outpouring of his love for humanity? In this case, more profoundly, Jesus' proclamation continues. The Father responds:

> You have it right, 'blessed are those who have ears to
> hear.'

Father, could it be that such discrepancy confuses the
faithful?

> I understand your concern, but you must recall how the
> Church was defined by the blood sacrifice of my Son.
> Although not established according to my intention, his
> gift of love is realized, but the kingdom is not, and the
> pilgrimage continues. I do not abandon my people. I call
> them endlessly to the place of my heart.

The Question of Typology

When some theologians connect the dots for tightly knitting a
relationship between the Old Testament and Jesus the Messiah, it
raises questions. The "typology" intends to connect biblical
assertions to define a complete and uncontested biblical narrative.
The goal is to establish continuity between the Old Testament
understanding of sin and retribution with Jesus the Messiah.
Therefore, this attempt at continuity intends to affirm the meaning
of Jesus' cross as a sacrifice for humanity's sins. Such thinking
confuses the "Good News" of the kingdom Jesus proclaimed.

Again, a reminder that Paul's writings influenced the written
word of much of the New Testament scriptures. And no doubt, the
understanding was used also to link Old Testament precepts to the
cross of Christ.

For example, I reference the Old Testament metaphor "Like a
Lamb led to the slaughter" (Is 53:7). The same metaphor repeats in
the Acts of the Apostles 8:32-35. Many believe the prophecy of the

Old Testament points to Jesus as the Sacrificial Lamb five hundred years before the fact. Evidence suggests the writer of "Acts" is advancing Paul's storyline.

I am not at all denying Jesus' role as a Sacrificial Lamb. However, I am saying he is not a Sacrificial Lamb slain for the sake of our sins. In its original form, the metaphor in the Book of Isaiah refers to the nation of Israel and the slaughter they suffered at the hands of their enemies.

Although written five hundred years before Christ, the book is prophetic and in God's keeping. As such, the interpretations could easily apply to Jesus. However, once again, this derails the "Good News" of the kingdom Jesus proclaimed. Although a Lamb led to the slaughter, Jesus' intention was not to fulfill a prophecy for appeasing the Father.

On the contrary, Jesus led the way to glorify the Father. For those who followed him, there was no turning back. And even though they were slain, the love that built Jesus' Temple remains, and the path opens. Called to reignite the way, I declare that our love for God is God's glory. Yet still, for many, the past stands in the way.

Here is the fine line between Jesus' death understood for sin, and his cause for the kingdom of God. The Father's love is the foundation of Jesus' truth compromised by humanity's definitions of sin and repentance. The Father's love is first, before all else. In our world, however, the Father's love is often held back by laws and practices surrounding remedies for sin. In effect, God's love is trumped by instruments and measures that push people away. Such barriers injure the truth of the Father's heart.

No higher solution exists than to approach the Father with an open heart. The consequences of misunderstanding may appear as small, but the implications are enormous to the point of closing the gates Jesus opened.

Interestingly, make no mistake that Jesus talks about opening the gates. In truth, the Gate of the Father's heart was never closed. On the contrary, countless hearts close because precepts and remedies for sin exist that create guilt and shame flowing from fear. At the very least, those who do not feel worthy of God's approval are beyond counting.

I remember a young mother who approached me with a troubled heart concerning an act understood as a severe sin within the Church. When I directed her to a higher authority, her fear heightened. She did not follow through. From childhood to adulthood, her story was incredibly telling. The rules held her away from the Father's mercy.

I speak of her story because the example holds back the life of the kingdom Jesus proclaimed. Consider the cause for the Father's cry, "Why do you still persecute me?" We are the Father's children. Who suffers more for their children than their parents? The Father's cry is no different, except in unimaginable proportions.

Here, the negative effects of Paul's reasoning are on display, and the differences between Paul's foundation and the ground of Jesus are clearly revealed. Paul was busy managing the problem of sin to be worthy of God. On the other hand, Jesus' mission is to expose the open door to the Father's heart. The Father adds that:

> To love me is a choice and for living freely, but one
> must enter the door I open.

The rules and laws of men are proven to close the doors Jesus opens even to some who have ears to hear. Again, the reasons for the Father's haunting cry to echo through time.

God makes us in the dignity of God's image with no intention to be subject to laws and practices that identify with sin and judgment. Instead, Jesus directs us into the light. How do we expect to be free when exercising rules and practices that magnify sin and judgment? By doing so, we perpetuate the afflictions that build walls between the Father and us. To think that God would shape us to be all that we can be through instruments of fear is ironic. God is *Love* and through love only does God shape God's children. We have lost this treasure of God's truth!

We understand how some like the dark, and not all have ears to hear. Jesus says, "...nor will they say, 'Look, here it is!' or 'There it is!' For, in fact, the kingdom of God is among you" (Lk 17:21). As the scriptures allude, the kingdom's concept is hard to grasp; perhaps that is because its rise or fall depends on us.

Schism of Jesus' Truth

The Sword

Extraordinary in weight and size, I see the vision of a massive pully lifting high overhead a massive blade displaying the force of a ramming battleship. With a sudden and precise downward drive, the weapon rips into the trunk of the majestic tree. The strike is like thunder and splitting like lightning. Jesus continues:

Jesus' Throne but Not His Truth

> The Christian persecutions were coming to an end, although at a high cost. Free from living in hiding, the unfolding Church was not as I ordained. Rather, settling on the foundation of men, hence the unimaginable sword, illustrating the schism of my truth. The shattering was soon to surface in the differences among the developing Christian communities. When it came to the precepts laid down by the First Council, many believing in me disagreed, and at an unjust price.
>
> My truth is and always was about reigning in the kingdom of God. In everything I preached, in all my actions, I unfolded the light of a loving Father.

Knowledge of the Father was at the heart of my mission. You do not understand that the in-breaking of the Father's love is the in-breaking of the kingdom of God. Many say I am light to the world. My light was and always will be the light that shines on the Father's heart. Although the love by which I met humanity caught on fire, my light is dimmed by the reasoning of men.

A point came when Church laws created a defining line and with that, drew a line of defense. Because of their fears, the early officials thought to defend their posturing, as though the severing of one's ear was on my behalf. Unfortunately, the ramifications were much more severe and not to my benefit.

The price of killing those who differed in their rational views is a troublesome burden to carry in my name. More disconcerting, those considered to be heretical, did not deviate from my foundational truth: that I am the Son; and the Father's love is the fortress on which I stand.

Jesus is talking about the splintering of his truth, particularly concerning the one reason why he came. Hence, a schism that only he and the heavens could see and sadly, with anguish that he and the Father endured and soon to spread through time. Although many Catholics and Christians of various denominations today do not know its extent, they know somewhere, and somehow, something is broken. And if nothing else, even they undeniably give credit to the minds of men. Hence, the Church has a history of schisms and people migrating from one denomination to another. What was crucial to Jesus' truth that the founding fathers of our faith somehow missed?

Following the Decree of Religious Toleration 313 C.E., implemented under the rule of Emperor Constantine, the Christian communities came out of hiding. What happened next would soon initiate a dramatic turn of events. History's most glorious moment was about to be toppled by history's most disturbing.

The vision unveils a complicated era that propelled the Church's life to a point of no return. Historians commonly agree that the Edict of Religious Toleration opened the door to a historical turning point. Indeed, it was a grand shift, however, it's alarming to look back through centuries past and view the overarching ramifications of this change.

Of course, Christianity's newfound freedom was momentous, yet equally notable; it was a double-edged sword. In a grave sense, when considering Jesus' proclamation, it became a turning point downward. And, therefore, it's necessary to revisit the changes brought by this decree, although it's impossible to unpack every little detail of a long and tedious history of the Church. Although long and knotty, there are two critical events to consider. They are the "Edict of Milan," known as the "Edict of Religious Toleration" and the First Council of Nicaea that followed.

The first event concerns Emperor Constantine's Decree of Religious Toleration, declared in 313 C.E. Here, supposedly, marked the end of Christian bloodshed. In this sense, it was a crucial turning point for the sake of the struggling Church. However, the early Church fathers came out of hiding and with unfortunate differences. Not all Christians shared the same perspectives about the man-God Jesus. Of all things, they differed in their understanding of his human and divine nature. And now, the differences were becoming heated disagreements.

Divided by ideas concerning the "nature" and "will" of Jesus in relationship to the "nature" and "will" of God became a point of contention. Here was the human mind attempting to define the infinite mind of the Father and the Son. I am not saying this is without merit. However, since they found no common ground on which to build, the Spirit of the Father that Jesus proclaimed was absent from their process. When unable to build on common ground, the misfortune of a power struggle became inevitable.

History speaks of the early father's disagreements turning into disputes. Yet, here also unfolds the rupturing of Jesus' truth. Soon their differences turned them against each other and then became electrified by dictates and judgments of heresy.

Before the First Council, toward the end of the second century, Bishop Irenaeus had already developed a five-volume decree against heresies. Adding to his perspective, he declared that those opposed to his constructs were heretical and subject to exile and even death as an appropriate remedy. Well into the thirteenth century, even the great St. Thomas Aquinas wrote, "…heretics deserve not only to be separated from the Church by ex-communication but also to be severed from the world by death" (1225-1274 C.E.).[8] Fathers of the Church agreed, including St. Augustine of Hippo (354-430 C.E.).

Fathers of the First Council were posturing themselves no differently than Paul before his conversion, and like Paul, their zeal was for defending their beliefs in God. Of course, the unrest caused by their differences did not bode well with the emperor, who insisted on the Empire's unity. Constantine had an avid interest and role in Church function and development even when initiating the First

---

[8] Aquinas, St. Thomas *The Summa Theologica,* Second Part of Part Two, Question 11, Article 2, Question 3.

Council of Nicaea 325 C.E. This was a step that would have lasting effects on Church precepts and practices.

Remember, Constantine was a Roman Emperor, still paying homage to many gods, and as far as history is concerned, that never changed. The point demonstrates that Constantine's intent is not necessarily about honoring the God of Christians but instead seeking control over the Empire. Under his request, Christian officials convened for the first time for the sake of establishing unity. Although a noble cause, the principles were soon founded on the developing doctrines based on human reasoning.

From the start, Church officials did not reflect the martyrs' galvanized strength, and it was about to become evident at their First Council. Their arguments reflect Jesus' story about sheep without a shepherd. I don't seek to cast blame on them, but I say this to set the stage for revisiting the early Church fathers and their deliberations. I understand that creation is a wheel in progress but does that mean we ought not to look back to see where we have been to move forward in the present.

Intensely arguing amongst themselves at times, they tugged on each other's beards. They were not at all on solid footing but were divided due to intellectual differences. As I recall, Jesus taught his followers about faith in God and faith in oneself in relationship to the Father. These were not rational concepts. Hence, from the beginning, their intellectual disputes were not in keeping with the tenets of Christ.

Jesus guided his followers with precepts of faith for breeding trust in the Spirit of the Father with them. He put forth guidelines for prayer to nourish their hearts and souls. He did not lay down precepts to develop intellectual learning. Of course, this would be natural for humans, but this was not the foundation on which Jesus built.

Intellectual understanding may enhance the foundation, but here, dividing the foundation as the human intellect ventures into God's unlimited mind. Consequently, the Church fathers squeezed the extraordinary extent of God's love into a box. Here resides the grave error against the work of the Son. Although their intent may have been for a higher purpose, the brain's engine to get there is insufficient. Hence, revealing God's love is the reason why the Son came among men and women, "to begin with."

The Church father's differences meant little to God. The point was not about dissecting Jesus' nature but that the Messiah reveals God's love for his people. The question is about faith. Apparently, they reached no such ground on which to stand. As one can see at the First Council, they created a foundation built on the limits of human reasoning, and the effects have filtered through history. Jesus did not rely on academic precepts. Instead, he reveals the essence of the Father's heart who loves them. The mind of God is neither condemning nor the heart of God that loves the creation. Here are the solid foundations on which Jesus builds, yet his truth was crumbling. And with it, his Temple was caving in, meaning that the essence of the kingdom he proclaimed was slipping away from the hearts of men and women.

The Council sought to establish precepts on which they could agree. Unfortunately, they were about to develop definitions of the Church that would carry through history. When it was over, they were not in full agreement, nevertheless, they established what they understood as the Church's foundational dogmas and doctrines.

Consequently, Arius, a priest of Alexandria, was the first exiled for his belief, now labeled the Arianism heresy. He saw Jesus as created by the Father, and therefore not co-eternal or consubstantial (of the same substance) with the Father. As other differences emerged, the heresies continued to develop in number and momentum. Over time, the heresies built one on top of another with no solid grounding in Jesus' truth which eventually fell into an unreachable box.

Remember, many who claimed to be heretics loved the Father through the Son. They were not at the table for any other reason. As I write, my love for God is everything to me, and the reason my life is spent heartbroken over Jesus' truth falling short in many of today's churches. How much more the Father's heart who pleads, "Why do you still persecute me?" Intentionally or not, the children do not come, and God's sorrow is far more than mine.

The Father's Voice

> People do not realize my love for them, tell me, who is to blame? Did my Son fail to love, that I should be denied the fruits of his labor? His sacrifice was misplaced over two thousand years by many thrones that have not the wisdom he held in his heart.

Constantine immediately forbade any assembly of the heretics and began confiscating their public properties. Under Roman rule, Bishop Irenaeus' preamble for heresies and penalties soon became a standard part of Church life. Influenced by Roman constructs, the Church began to veer toward a militant approach while rapidly advancing on a foundation resembling the Roman structures of power and control.

The early fathers had forgotten that Jesus was a guiding light who halted Peter's aggression and restored the ear of Malchus. The groundwork was developing for a long era of confusion and disorder where those persecuted were about to become the persecutors. The Council laid down precepts understood as dogmas and doctrines of the Church. To differ, question, or refute those doctrines, came with the costly charge of heresy. In effect, offenders were subject to judgments, punishments, and persecutions.

At this point, the Church was bound to the state, and the state assisted the Church in its declarations. Intending to keep its people in unison, the Church grew in defense of its newly sanctioned precepts. In retrospect, the newly emerging partnership was about to enter a new era of chaos under the banner of a painfully misguided Church.

Before long, the tortures carried over to anyone deemed a threat to the faith. History demonstrates how broadly prejudice spread. In the showing of the "Torch," Jesus says, "Do not let anyone fool you, the 'torch of terror' burned for another fifteen centuries." He is emphatic about noting that the bloodshed did not end with the Edict of Religious Toleration, as one might think. One may sense the gravity beneath Jesus' words, because the precepts he stood against were being doled out from his throne.

Many refer to this era as the "Dark Ages," while some recall it as an age of Christians persecuting Christians. When looking back through history, some may say that "Okay, there were heretics who were severely punished, but that is behind us now." Jesus is telling another story.

I recall a passage in the Gospel of Mark. In it, Jesus offered important clues about the kingdom of God to a scribe. The scribe began by asking Jesus which commandment is first above all. Jesus told him that the first is to love God with all that you are, and then he added, the second is to love your neighbor as yourself. The scribe favored Jesus' response. And then Jesus revealed a significant clue about the kingdom of God when saying to him, "You are not far from the kingdom of God" (Mk 12:34).

It makes me wonder how we have missed Jesus' explicit message. Those who say, "the persecutions are behind us now, or it was not so bad," make me think about how distant they are from the kingdom of God.

As documented, the First Council drew a line in the sand. If anyone spoke differently about their precepts, they were subject to judgment and persecution. The outcome was not necessarily the intention of the emperor at that time. However, as it happened, he did nothing to stop it. Instead, he was more apt to see it as a credit to his success. In retrospect, much like Saul, the Church would eventually adopt the title, "Defenders of the Faith."

Jesus came in peace to gather the Father's children, not to destroy them. How easily we can see that his message is snowed under by the reasoning of men. Although the truth hurts, these visions are for mining the burial grounds of Jesus' lost treasures, not for blame or more hurt. They are meant to refuel the soul with life's most precious gift. Jesus puts it another way:

> Understanding what went wrong is essential; that is the
> purpose. Otherwise, where is the starting point?

Again, I turn to Paul's work that influenced the scriptures and the precepts of the Church. The Nicene Creed gives evidence of Paul's leverage (1Cor 15:3-4). To begin, Jesus was not hung up on chasing sins. Instead, he led people to a higher standard for moving them beyond their sins.

On the other hand, Paul squeezed the meaning of Jesus' cross into the constructs of the "Old Tradition," and the kingdom of God was pushed off to the afterlife. What little else Paul suggested concerning God's kingdom relates to lawful preparations for maintaining "citizenship" in heaven. Nonetheless, Paul's confusion is hard to hide since the kingdom remains a place in the afterlife.

For Paul, sin is the earthshaking barrier between God and us due to the fallen human nature that cannot rise above sin. In effect, he contests a corrupted world of people due to the sin of Adam. In effect, he denies God made man and woman and saw them as good. In retrospect, Paul declares that only through the sacrifice of God's Son can the fallen human be saved from God's wrath. His focus is on sin and a defective creation, and we depend entirely on Jesus' cross to release us from the pains of a dark world. From this perspective, Paul unravels the meaning of Jesus' cross.

But is this what Jesus and the Father intended? And what does that say about the dignity of the human? Although Paul talks about living as citizens of heaven now, his theology still flows from the ground of sin. Hence, he is not without a host of rules to follow. In effect, we must patiently and effectively bide our time before we are set free from the pitfalls of this life. Is this God's plan? Or is there something more to the human that Jesus saw in people? And did he not proclaim a different paradigm considering who God is and who we are as people of God?

As it is, Paul puts the cart before the horse; Jesus does not. God's love is first before all else; that is what genuinely frees us and ignites us to become the Temples of the kingdom that Jesus proclaimed is with us now. The Father does not expect that we would love an angry or punishing God! Here is a stumbling block for Paul, and I have witnessed many good and faithful people stumbling needlessly.

Although Paul's claims are highly extravagant and noteworthy, his wisdom does not match that of Jesus. At times, paradoxically, Paul's deliveries foster judging attitudes that are not a product of the paradigm for which Jesus stood.

Realistically, to place oneself in the mindset of our ancestors is impossible. Nonetheless, Paul's outspoken nature gets to the crux of his shortcomings. Do not forget, Paul had only the scriptures of "Old." He is the first writer of the New Testament, and clearly, he was at odds with the apostles. Furthermore, many believe Paul felt he knew better than the Twelve. Interestingly, this notion only holds up if the kingdom of God is not a part of the equation! Connecting the dots, the visions ahead unveil the full breadth of God's kingdom.

History continued, and so did the divides within all Christendom. Some Christians see eye to eye, and sometimes not; sadly, some cast stones, and others are more concerned about appeasing a disappointed God. One might think that history has turned a blind eye to the many blows to the foundation Jesus laid down. According to Jesus and the Father, indeed, it has! Perhaps not intentionally, but that is where we are today.

Many are to blame for things going wrong or falling short. I know God is not about pointing fingers. Still, the notion is unsettling that from the depths of their hearts, the martyrs died sharing in the genuine love of the Father. Yet, the treasure of Jesus' truth did not make it to the First Council's table.

Although so little, if anything, is said about them, I do not deny that the martyrs' love reached us. I say so because their blood is remembered at liturgies, and the faithful are aware of their extraordinary acts of love for God and God's love for them. Perhaps a silent tradition, and their memory lives beneath the surface. How sad to think the most sacred treasure of Jesus' truth passed away with them.

Ground of Fear

Grim Reaper

The light vanishes from the room. Piercing the shadows, a vision of a grim reaper appears. His dark garment madly flows in the chilling air. The hollowed eyes are peeping through an overstated hood that spooks with its shivering skull. Disproportionately huge limbs protruding from the bellowing sleeves fall to its sides. Here, with elbows bent and arms shifting away from the garment, it displays immense claw-like hands. Jesus explains:

Fall of the Kingdom

> The vision of the 'grim reaper' is not a pleasant depiction, but rather a showing of death. I am not talking about physical death. Instead, the end of my kingdom is brought about by the hands of those who stand in its way. Let us call them the Grim Reapers of the kingdom. They are those who see less of my truth and replace it with seats of power and prestige.

When turning to the showing of the "Torch," Jesus is emphatic about underscoring the long reign of persecutions that continued into the early nineteenth century. Hundreds of years tell the bitter truth that the Church was not standing on Jesus' foundation, but rather wading in the fears of men. One must question the early Church fathers who defined the judgments, punishments, and executions. It gives me no delight to give voice to the bloodshed and butcheries that were beyond heretical. Frankly, I pause when sadly saying the tortures were diabolical. And how many Vicars of Christ ignored Jesus' words to Peter when telling him to put down his sword? Yet, on this foundation, the Church stands. Jesus talks about building on solid ground, but it is sorrowfully missing.

I recall the words of a prominent Bishop who stated, "It took us fifteen hundred years to get into this mess. It will take us a lot longer to get out of it." At the time, I did not know what he meant. I do now, and although it will take longer, the bigger question is, what will it take to begin? Perhaps unscrambling the past is a start.

Apologies for the past are not enough to change the foundation on which the Church is built. Although seeing more into God's love is good, however, climbing less the ladders of human reasoning that build on the fears of our forefathers. Still, the fires of the past burn. Although not at stake, they are the fires of guilt, shame, judgments, and fear that scorch the soul's life. The ashes have not yet settled.

Most believe the foundation of the Church is vested in God's absolute truth and founded on solid ground. However, within little more than a decade, the early fathers' dictates of condemnation reigned over God's heart. On the other hand, Jesus' message was not etched in writing. It did not have to be! His truth is beyond the limits of human reasoning. Instead, Jesus' message was enshrined in the hearts of his followers.

Here, I recall the story about a divine vision etched in the heart of the great Thomas Aquinas that halted his intellectual pursuit. The most renowned Doctor of the Church, Thomas began teaching at the

University of Paris in about 1250. As history reveals, the work of the Saint was monumental. Eventually, his philosophy dominated the western world. As recent as the year 1950, Pope Pius XII, in the encyclical Humani Generis (Of the Human Race), endorsed the Thomistic philosophy as the assured ground for Roman Catholic doctrine while discouraging any divergence from it.

Although Paul lays down some groundwork for what is natural and unnatural (Rom 1:18-32), Thomas's legendary work on the "natural law" takes it to another level. In his tome, "The Summa Theologica," St. Thomas composed a rational argument regarding homosexual behavior. The "peccata contra naturam" (sins against nature) condemns such acts as grievous sins of lust because they are "contrary to right reason" as well as natural law. Through common reasoning, the Saint precludes that the intended order of sexual union is for procreation. Any human acts against the order of human reason are considered sinful.

As understood, the foundation was cast for the Church to establish its vision concerning matters of human sexuality, including artificial contraception

St. Thomas clearly states that sin is an act "against the order of reason." Given the reasoning of "natural law," the act of cross-dressing as a man was the lever used to deny Joan of Arc her innocence of heresy. On the other hand, a courtroom bursting with educated clergymen thought it natural to execute a nineteen-year-old virgin by burning her at stake.

Without doubting the brilliance of the Saint, the fact is that no matter how intelligent any human being may be, the reasoning of the mind cannot supersede the logic of divine love. To date, the Church refutes its posture on the natural law; however, little if anything has changed, if only the rhetoric.

Jesus' vision stretched far beyond the reasoning of the mind. If this were not so, the Twelve Apostles would not have had such difficulty understanding. To love one's enemies does not configure with the mind's reasoning. Reducing attraction and intimacy to the mind's limits also reduces the richer images of God from which we are made.

Interestingly, St. Thomas never completed his enormous philosophical project, the "Summa Theologica," not by default but on purpose. After celebrating Mass, the Saint received a vision. Shortly afterward, he was unwilling to continue his work. The only conclusion one can draw regards his response to his colleague, father Reginald. Thomas explained that all he had written was meaningless compared to what he saw.[9]

Although remaining silent, could he have seen anything more or less than a vision of divine love? Perhaps, one of the Sacred Heart of Jesus standing among those burned at stake.

Heresy does not exist but in the minds of men. The varying notions of heresy were small compared to the grounding truth of the Father's divine love. I look back in time and see how the heresies come from those who make their claims. Who are the heretics? Today, people are not slain, although countless souls are still under fire. How many do not know or deny the wounds inflicted on the souls of the Father's children? And the Father's plea is to know, "Why do you still persecute me?" Where is the Good Shepherd's rule, who speaks of God's care for his flock and guides them without imposing heavy demands on them?

---

[9] Turner, Denys *Thomas Aquinas: A Portrait*, Chapter One, The Silence of the Saint, Yale University Press, New Haven & London, 2013 (Chapter One, pages 40-46).

Looking back on history, one may have little doubt that God would circumvent the work of the great Saint. Thomas had a soul awakening to discover that intellect cannot grasp the wisdom of divine love. He came not merely to the end of his work but also to a new horizon. Consequently, he was left to ponder a higher perspective.

The change of heart is the more extraordinary legacy of the Saint, less his words inscribed in manuscripts but a vision that changed his life. Here, we are left to ponder with him the divine wisdom that altered his thought pattern. In the same way, divine truth was the apostles' stumbling block, not because they were uneducated. On the contrary, divine reasoning exists beyond the reaches of the mind. From God's view, we are here to flourish, yet how can we grow when stuck on a ground distant from the outlook of the Father's heart?

Intellect can only take us so far. The question is not how well we have learned, "but how we have loved which matters." Beyond any doubt, the Saint had a powerful mind wrought with good intentions. Conversely, because of his intellectual influence, a fair portion of Thomas's work is a mighty instrument for closing many books on love. If our knowledge does not support a more meaningful understanding of love, then what value does it have in God's eyes?

Again, the problems the Church faces are beyond apologies for the past. Instead, to actualize the higher vision of divine love for growth and resolve. We are the ones who narrow the gates with laws, precepts, and judgments that stand in *Love's* way. The centuries have cloaked the kingdom of God in a veil of darkness. Jesus' intent was, is, and will never be to judge or point fingers but to lift the darkness that hides the full picture of God's truth. He did not commission judges. In the Gospel of John, Jesus commissions twelve way-showers of God's love because they were shown divine love. Before his departure, Jesus sent forth his apostles with this commendation:

> I give you a new commandment, that you love one another. Just as I have loved you, you also should love one another. By this everyone will know that you are my disciples, if you have love for one another (Jn 13:34-35).

I am one for making peace, and the work is immensely challenging. It pains me to disclose the unfortunate truth. I take no delight in that, but I cannot deny the Father's words, "I paid a great price in the blood of my Son. Why do you still persecute me?" One need not listen to me. Listen to the Father's plea, and decide who speaks and to whom he is speaking.

Some will say that God does not feel. I felt those words. Furthermore, how does persecution feel? God speaks to his Church: "Why do you still persecute me?" As written, he experiences the pain of his children. Jesus says, "...whatever you do to another, you do to me."

As with the Son, God's Spirit is an intimate part of who we are, and he is, after all, the author of life. We talk about respecting life but do not see the past's undoing that continues to hinder God's children.

We may not be burning anyone at stake, but fear of God still taints Church precepts and practices. And fear is not God's way of doing things. God does not, will not, and cannot go against the grain of God's nature. Therefore, the Father does not shape men and women to be who God desires them to be, with that which is not of God, and fear is not of God. God is *Love*, and fear has no room.

Here, I must unpack a learning experience while in my fourth year of Seminary College. Given the freedom to develop a thesis of choice, we were to complete a fifty-page research paper. Guided by my mentor, an awesome priest, he overlooked my query concerning the contemporary German philosopher, Martin Heidegger. Looking back, I see a clear thread that led me to gather more pieces of a giant puzzle. And here is a central portion of the big picture.

Heidegger's work "Being and Time" filters down to developing a "ground for Being." He hypothesizes that death is the ground for "Being" in time. Masterfully, he articulates his views through the idea that we live on a horizon, and during that timeline, one must make of oneself all that one can be. However, it's easy to recognize the severe pitfalls within his thinking because it leaves the playing field wide open. Consequently, many believe his work encouraged the development of Hitler's Totalitarian agenda.

I have struggled to know how his work might relate to Jesus' cross, because if anyone left us a ground for "Being," it was Jesus. And for years, the question came up. Nonetheless, the answer I sought did not. Yes, forgiveness is through his cross, but then was it only to pick ourselves up and sin no more? I feel less a ground for "Being," only a basis to get us through another day. It was not painting a complete picture, and I could not get my full heart around it.

Not that I do not appreciate and love that Jesus would die for our sins, but that there is more to the magnitude of his cross. Many receive forgiveness, yet hardly if ever feel accepted in God's eyes, and they are thirsty for more. Then, we are left to stumble and fall. Sometimes we fall back three steps, take one step forward, and the scenario repeats. How many feel a path they walk and can hardly complete?

The path opens when understanding that the in-breaking of the kingdom is at once the in-breaking of the Father's love through Jesus Christ. And the ground that Jesus came to place us on becomes incredibly clear. He spent his life preaching and teaching the kingdom of God through his every word and action. He taught us that God is Father, and then he continued to put a face on God, revealing the Father's unimaginable love. Hence, the Father's love is our solid ground for "being." Jesus did not have to die to fulfill his mission, but his cross magnified the depths of the Father's love and for the sake of God's children. God knows the enemy is fear, and Jesus came to quell that enemy.

However, his truth is lost in the mayhem and fears following his cross. Jesus' mission was to live fully in the image of God. That was his purpose; that he would set us free from our fears and into the arms of an incomprehensible loving Father. Here, unveils the secret strength of the martyrs.

That is not to say freedom comes without guidelines. However, they aren't parameters grounded in laws and rules that create judgment and more fears. Instead, the ground of being unfolds within the reaches of the Father's love. Wherefore, with God's love comes the freedom to experience all that God gives according to the measure of love we are reflecting. So, it is that service to others is service to God and the kingdom Jesus proclaims. However, how is one to take the first step, especially beginning with self-love, without the truth of God's love?

Deep within, I know the early Church fathers were brilliant, but their fears got the best of them. Standing firmly against the test of time, they held strongly to their views. Etched in writing, their fears drafted a new dawn of terror that continued for fifteen hundred years. And God knows the enemy of the soul. If only we were to garner our human reasoning and bathe ourselves in the heart of our loving Father, we could indeed be the kingdom Jesus proclaims.

Fifteen hundred years of Church history paints a clear picture that when Church laws and rules flow from the fears of men, the outcome is destructive to the soul's life and the Body of Christ. God knows nothing is more threatening to the soul than our fears, and so he sent his Son.

Perhaps humankind is not ready, and we will only be when grasping the difference between divine wisdom and human reasoning. Laws, rules, and practices that create hurt and judgments are not grounds for being. Instead, they are grounds that hold us away from the kingdom Jesus proclaims. They are grounds that keep us far from the Father's heart and prevent believers from reaching for the love God wishes us to reach.

As opposed to demonstrating our faith, we have learned to defend our faith, and the rules we defend often stand in the way of love. Indeed, God is pure *Love*, and we are not. I say that because God does not need us to defend the faith but to be faithful. God's love is the mightiest plan to protect and to gratify, and in God's image, we are made. Undoubtedly, many are lost, and the road is weary. Often, I wonder if we will find our way.

Do not be fooled! I love the people of the Church. I miss the parishioners I served, from the youngest to the oldest. I know there are uncountable good priests and those of religious orders, and many I love. I respect and admire the educators who taught me, and my gratitude will remain. Honestly, it pains me to be the messenger. However, what good would it do for God and God's people to withhold what God places in my heart?

My ambition is not to throw stones at anyone but to address the painfully broken foundation. The foundation is still riddled with laws and precepts that flow from men's fears rather than the Father's love. To replace it with the ground of the Father's heart is what "Jesus would do."

Today, many believe the Church fathers' truths are God's absolute truth and are founded on solid ground. However, within little more than a decade, the early fathers picked up their pens to write condemning litanies that continue to weigh on the Father's heart.

In retrospect, we have adopted the pedestal of Paul and far less the ground of the Son. Our sin is not what narrows the way, but our lack of compassion overruled by our propensity to judge. God does not need our defense. God wants our love and not by fear or force, subtle or loud, but by choice drawn from the example personified in the Son.

The Father Concludes

> I offer my message of realization. Realizing that not all is as it seems. All is not bad, and all is not good. Creation is someplace in the middle, and the end times speeding closer. You see yourselves what falls to the left, and what falls to the right.
>
> The advance of my Son's truth caused a collision with those on the left and the right. The rest is history. Now we are here. Yet, the fork in the road is no less a divide than it was more than fifteen hundred years past. Those left and right are clear in their pursuit and the ground from which they operate.
>
> In this work, you have a gift for opening your eyes to choose a better world. Indeed, I am with you, and those 'who have ears to hear' and a heart to listen, you

will find your place with me. That is the gift. Once again, the way opens to me as once opened by my Son.

Jesus & Paul / The Wall Between Them

The Airship

Paused in time, I receive the portentous showing of the "Airship." Mysteriously, the monstrous zeppelin sails before me. Wishing the craft was a phantom, I could only watch in anticipation. A vessel of ghosts, laggardly voyaging through the virgin blue sky, the perilous arch turns toward me. Dark in color and faceless, my eyes widened to see the atrocity drawing near, then suddenly erupting. A blazing inferno corrupting the sky, unleashing gusting waves of scorching heat, the fiery debris and splintering ashes bursting in every direction. Then, all I could see was the blurring red horizon overshadowed by the darkness of pulsing black clouds. Jesus reveals:

Paul's Vision

> The Airship is symbolic of the direction in which Paul's theology set sail the Church. You can see that indeed the Church imploded after the First Council and how long its implosion burned its way through history. I give this image to clarify why it would shatter with such high intensity.

As you understand, the kingdom I revealed centers on the Father's love. Paul did not know me. Paul only knew that I died preaching in the Father's name. Shown the mercy of God, Paul realized forgiveness, which Paul acknowledges. However, he did not understand why, and that he was standing in the way of my truth. Instead, he defines his experience through the lens of the Judaic Tradition.

As a result, his weaknesses were like an anchor that continued to haunt him. Henceforth, he talks about his sinful nature that he cannot escape. Admitting he does not do what he should, he views himself as a slave to sin as though two people live within him.

Paul defines his human nature by the laws that bind him far less than the Father who loves him. The difference may sound subtle, but the void is immeasurable. He does not know the incomprehensible wisdom of God voiced by Jesus. Paul said, "Now if I do what I do not want, I agree that the law is good. But in fact, it is no longer I that do it, but sin that dwells within me" (Rom 7:16-17). Paul's teaching is not the voice of the kingdom Jesus proclaims.

Paul did not understand the full impact of God's saving love except to see that he is forgiven for what he had done. As such, although he experiences God's mercy, he is never entirely resolved.

The scenario is much like what happens in many of the confessional forums of today. A person may receive God's forgiveness, but they still hang onto something they have not fully resolved. Like Paul, they have a sense that whatever befalls them will occur again. When all is said and done, what is missing is God's acceptance, which goes beyond forgiveness. To be forgiven is one thing, while to be accepted is another. How many people, like Paul, still feel like sinners who are not accepted?

I do not intend to judge Paul but to gratify the truth in Christ. Rather, I laud Paul for being who he was and giving all that he had to make a difference. However, as history played out, Paul did not get Jesus' purpose right. The apostle is unable to fully embrace himself and see within himself the image of God. Paul's posturing is not the way of God, or the kingdom Jesus proclaims. Instead, Paul lived as one who did not have the ears to hear.

Paul's Influence

When the First Council instituted what they had in writing, evidence suggests Paul's theology was at the helm. Even today, when theologians want to look at doctrines of sin, they go to the Letters of Paul. In them, you will find the "New Adam" in Jesus because all descend unto death through Adam, while in Jesus, all rise to justification and life. Hence, Paul's theology portends resolving the Old Testament problem with sin.

Paul defines original sin in his letter to the Romans 5:12-14, which is captured in the precepts of the Nicene Creed, 325CE: "We believe in one baptism for the remission of sins." For Paul, all people are united with Adam's sin, and only through Jesus Christ, the new Adam, are we free from original sin. And here, it reflects Paul's influence on the founding precepts of Church doctrine.

Although Paul did not define baptism in Christ as the means to be redeemed by Jesus' blood. However, it's evident that the early Church interpreted the need to be free of Adam's sin and baptism was their answer.

In recent years, the Catholic Church renewed its definition of baptism. Accordingly, the effects of baptism are for initiation into the community of believers. Nonetheless, many mothers continue to worry about the problem of original sin while, on the other hand, churches seek to be born again in Christ. The point here is not about how one is received into communion with God or Jesus, but to demonstrate Paul's weight on church theology.

Jesus did not represent a wrathful God. Instead, a loving God whose love is saving. By the time New Testament writings came to the surface, it's hard to deny that Paul's perception of sin influenced New Testament theology and the development of Church doctrine.

The Mayhem

Jesus is emphatic about revealing the extent of the "reign of terror" from beginning to end because of the grave error against his truth and most certainly expressed in the blood that continued to spill for centuries in his name.

At the start, Christians were under siege, and the books of the New Testament were in various locations and stages of storytelling, gathering, and writing. Sifting through the centuries, we have extensive knowledge about when they were written and those who wrote them. However, disagreements among theologians and scholars continue.

Though interesting to note, they tend to agree when considering the dating of Paul's letters which predate the writings within the New Testament, including the Gospels. His influence on the development of the written word is highly conceivable given the ancient process and duration of time. Who can deny that Paul's precepts forged the doctrines of the First Council?

In consideration of the developing Church, shortly after the First Council, in 330 C.E., Constantine commissioned the scholar and early father of the Church, Bishop Eusebius, to complete fifty versions of the biblical texts. He is also known as St. Jerome (in Latin, Eusebius Hieronymus), to whom Augustine raised a red flag in a letter of concern about Paul's "dishonor to Peter at Antioch."

At Constantine's request, Eusebius took charge of the task. Questions about their development are unanswered. Although the impetus was for unifying the early Christian communities, we do not know the guidelines for advancing the sacred texts.

Certainly, discernment was in place, with evidence pointing to Paul's theology as the rule of thumb. The entire process is under debate to this day.

However, most conceivably when attempting to understand God's incomprehensible love, such is the reason the apostles had difficulties embracing Jesus' teachings. Even the truth unfolding in this work may be challenging for some. The truth is that Jesus came with a message, and I question how it was missed, and how many are missing it. Reverting to Jesus in the synagogue, recall the passage again when he read from the prophet Isaiah in Luke's Gospel.

'The Spirit of the Lord is upon me, because he has anointed me to bring good news to the poor. He has sent me to proclaim release to the captives and recovery of sight to the blind, to let the oppressed go free, to proclaim the year of the Lord's favor.'

And he rolled up the scroll, gave it back to the attendant, and sat down. The eyes of all in the synagogue were fixed on him. Then he began to say to them, 'Today this scripture has been fulfilled in your hearing' (Lk 4:18-21).

Jesus did not say the "good news" was fulfilled through his sacrifice or ascending to the Father. Instead, he stated the good news of God's favor arises in your hearing today! Jesus did not speak of doctrines about sin or judgment. Instead, Jesus avowed he did not come to condemn. Furthermore, he added, "Do not judge, so that you may not be judged" (Mt 7:1). Jesus' doctrines are about love, forgiveness, healing, and liberation, and these are the gifts of God he is sent to satisfy.

He was against laws and practices that create judgments. Consequently, Paul's jurisprudence mirrors the problems of old codes. Even though Paul stated that Jesus' cross supersedes the law, he did not understand the new paradigm Jesus set into motion. He does not interpret an accurate picture of Jesus' life and teachings. Instead, Paul fixated on Jesus' death on the cross for our sins. Consequently, Paul's theology created a platform for judging others, which does not align with Jesus' truth. When understanding the kingdom of God that Jesus proclaimed, Paul's views are far less speculation but identifiable misconceptions.

Jesus pushed the "Old" codes aside. He does not judge. Instead, Jesus points to the transformative light of the Father's love. Paul was not equipped to understand what is beyond his mind's grasp. I have little doubt Paul was confused by his faults and fears when he encountered the love that altered his path. However, as smart as Paul was, his reasoning did not align with the wisdom of God's intent for humanity.

I do not suggest that Paul was all wrong. However, Paul missed the essential point. He took the reins believing he had it right and courageously set out to undo what he could not. Many think he succeeded, while many feel betrayed and hurt by the God of Christians. Indeed, I believe the churches are by God's ordination. However, something is wrong, and the full message of Jesus' saving truth hides beneath the ruins of history. Father, I believe you wished for a Church to hold up your name, but not as conceived.

> Of course, you do not have to apologize. Human free will comes with much unpredictability, which is part of the gift and awesomeness of humanity. Your choices have ramifications. However, you see the downside as well. All is not lost. Many love the Father and the Son. However, they are not free to be who I desire them to be. Instead, they are grasping for heaven as opposed to creating heaven on earth. The gift of free will is much more significant to behold.

Jesus affirmed the first two commandments are the greatest. And what are they, if not rooted in the love of God and love for one another? These intentions cannot effectively be a command but a two-way street involving God and humankind. The premise of love alone is a divine precept shedding light on the ground of the kingdom.

Jesus came to unleash the fullness of the Father's eternal promise of love. This alone sets the soul free. Here too, is the ground of the Father's doctrine for all life, and it comes with a choice. But how can one choose wholeheartedly when the residues of mayhem still linger to fog the distance between God and humans?

The dichotomies that follow are not to judge the apostle but set the stage for magnifying the higher ground on which Jesus stood. They create a pedestal for visualizing Jesus' significance and illuminating the human spirit.

Jesus & Paul / The Wall Between Them

I. Paul perceives the fallen human nature. Jesus perceives the human and divine nature.

II. Paul weighs in on sins of the flesh. Jesus weighs in on the intentions of the heart.

III. Paul places heavy burdens. Jesus' burden is light.

IV. Paul's perceptions hinge on the fears of our ancestors. Jesus' perceptions hinge on the ground of the Father's love.

V. Paul does not know God's nature. Jesus put a face on the nature of God.

VI. Paul develops a platform for judging. Jesus develops a platform for loving our enemies.

VII. Paul personifies divine law, a way of doing in time. Jesus personifies divine love, a way of being in time.

VIII. Paul confuses reasoning about faith and good works. Jesus exemplifies the depth of God's love that does not confuse.

IX. Paul emphasizes what God did for us. Jesus emphasizes who God "is" to us.

X. Paul proclaims the "Good News" of Jesus' cross. Jesus proclaims the "Good News" of the kingdom of God.

XI. Paul pushes the kingdom of God into the afterlife. Jesus unveils the kingdom of God with us now.

XII. Paul does not know the kingdom of God. Jesus' life centered on the kingdom of God.

Paul yoked Jesus' truth to the Old Testament standards based on sin and punishment. Paul correlated his beliefs and fears with our ancestors' perceptions of sin and God's punishment. In retrospect, he connected our ancestors' unresolved problem of sin and God's punishment to Jesus' cross. Here, Paul developed a logical solution for Jesus' cross based on the Jewish mindset concerning sacrifices in exchange for God's favor. Hence, he understood Jesus as the

Father's sacrifice for our sins. Let us not forget Abraham's story and the near sacrifice of his son.

Paul's language reflects the Old Testament prophets when claiming he was set apart since birth to preach the Gospel. Today, some believe he was set apart from the Twelve to the extent that he was more capable of leading. Father, how might we better understand?

The Father's Voice

> To understand is not complicated. Paul was a zealous man and his ego big, and so he thought his heart was for God. As you can see, the apostle did not get that right when slaughtering my children. The one thing Paul got right was my presence, but he relied on his rational views. I do not force my will on anyone. That would mean nothing to me. I gained his attention but did not order what he must or must not do. Paul acknowledged my presence and sometimes nudging, but he still saw things his way.
>
> Paul did not hear. As I said, he did not have ears to hear as much as he thought. And do not forget, no one in today's world can understand Paul's mind and heart who lived centuries ago. I did not choose him to slay anyone; any more than I chose him to override the gift of my Son's proclamation.

Am I right to think that many would hear your voice, or nudge if they were open and closely listening?

You live within the context of a noisy world, and many fall into a system of prayer, work, and play. Although not bad, the noise does not fit well with my voice and nudging because most are content to believe meeting me on the other side. The truth is that the other side many speak of is not why you are here. Instead, you are here to create on earth that which you await. The problem resides in a belief forged much too long ago. Hence, the cry within the pages of this book. I am to be heard now and for the greater good of humanity.

Sometimes the messages are overwhelming, and I am without words, and I must pause for reflection, at times for days or weeks. Other times my heart drops, and I fall to my knees, until I am ready to press on but always diving deeper into the *Love* embracing all creation.

PART 3

Where We Are Now

Misnomers of Men

Beyond the Misconception

Crashing Snowball

I see the viewing of a snowball rolling down a mountainside. Although futile, I think of stopping it in the spirit of urgency. Building in mass, the snowball's speed and size grows faster and larger until crashing through trees and toppling what appears to be a beautifully constructed lodge. Jesus continues:

God Given Human Nature

> That is how life plays out for most. You move along and grow old. The older you are, the faster time passes. The more responsibility, the more worry, and it continues to expand. Everything expands, and in its momentum, you can get spiritually lost in the way life happens.
>
> You must take time! Two thousand years have gone by, and many have not taken the time to read between the lines. Buying into systems of beliefs that are like print on a page is much too common. Many receive it, accept it, and run with life! Some pose questions, but because the untruth has snowballed for so long, you no longer have the time to complete the

answers. Now, the misconception of my truth is seeded deeply within the hearts and souls of men and women.

What makes better sense, that I came to save you or that I came to teach you to build? What have you been creating? How have you been saved, and from what have I saved you? Have I opened the gates of Paradise? Yet, you know that is a myth, a likely story. To say that humanity is fallen may be easy, but do you know where you have been? It would seem that from the beginning, you are here due to the Father's wrath. Hence, the suggestion is that I saved you from the Father's temper. Yet, I came to tell you that the Father is a loving Father and that is the good news of the kingdom; the good news on which to build. Based on this fact alone, how can the former make sense?

I know the puzzle of creation that most are unable to complete with limited mind and vision. Does it make sense that I came to lift you from the burden of the Father's wrath? Or that my cross is to appease his anger? To do so would only assert the matter of his wrath, hence, a negligent contradiction.

To lay down my life was a measure of sacrifice, demonstrating the depth of the Father's good intentions for humanity. The Father's intent was and will always be to draw his children closer to his side and never to push the human family away with the weight of heavy burdens.

Often, to fully understand what Jesus is conveying in both the visions and his discourses takes me a while, sometimes days, weeks, or even months, although they always become clear. My inability to define the building demolished by the snowball muddled my perception. Because the structure is unique, I contemplated its significance. Indeed, my first thought was a church structure, but I could not verify that. I began to think that maybe a cabin or home, or better still, a lodge that is carefully nestled in a scenic location. Puzzling me, I put the idea on the shelf until the meaning came to me that the Temple Jesus built is not necessarily recognized in many of today's churches, signifying that something vital is missing.

We are the creators of humanity's fall from the beginning according to Adam and Eve's sin. In its original form, it was just a story. Created by our ancestors, the myth explains the tensions they suffered. Hence, the "Snowball" imagery compares how the story's tension magnifies through time. And eventually, through a broken history of events, it topples the Temple Jesus built. Unfortunately, we do not have the ground of the kingdom Jesus proclaimed to understand the difference and to therefore validate our God-given divine human nature.

In effect, although we know the story is a myth, we do not know where else to turn for answers. Instead, we are still captives of the same saga that defines our fallen ways. Here is why Jesus refers to the story of paradise lost and raises the question, "You know of the myth, a likely story. Yet, you do not know from where you came." And adding, "What is more sensible, that I came to save you from God's wrath or that I came to teach you to build?"

How strange that for so long many remain distant from God and not by God's will. God's passion is impeded by the darkness of falsehood and fear. I surmise that sooner or later; his anguish will be revealed. And so, his voice calls out, "I paid a great price in the blood of my Son. Why do you still persecute me?" My motivation for doing this work springs from the Father's love crying out in sorrow. I can hardly express the magnitude of God's loving nature.

The Church's broken foundation is an example of God's truth inscribed as a print on a page. Here, we limit the unlimited Father, and the doctrines do not change. Instead, they are understood as divine truth etched in stone. Consequently, many are stuck and do not know how to make necessary changes because they believe God is unchangeable and defined by limited definitions. The reality is that God's truth does not change only to expand beyond the limits of human reasoning. We are a work in progress and are reaching for an unlimited God. Etching God's truth in stone has stood in the way of our emotional and spiritual progress by suppressing the wisdom and intent of an eternally loving Father.

The Father's Voice

> In truth, no man is equipped to claim divine authority over another, especially to etch my truth in stone. I understand the human need, but enough is enough. I am an infinite mystery not to be captured on a tablet, but to be expressed through the hearts of my people.

How do you explain your divine authority?

You know how I explain, please say it as you know it.

Jesus says not to lord authority over another, and his authority is unmatched. His divine authority was a means to lead the way, not to demand or dominate another, but to show the way.

> Is that not etched in your heart? You know the way, and you are chosen to lead the way.

Why is it so hard? Do we, as leaders in faith, understand the compassion of the Son, or do we deny it?

> Indeed, many have been in denial for far too long and many come to believe in the authority handed to them. Be sure many at the same time honor the authority as it should be, but at the root, the echo of time continues to hold steady a course that errs from my truth.

We talk about Jesus as our Savior who liberates the human family. I know this is true, but as Jesus illustrates, the full treasure of truth was not passed on to us. In every word and action, our Savior is, and always has been, the supreme manifestation of the Father's love. Jesus liberates us through the light of God's love, which alone sets us free.

Even so, God's calling is a free choice. Though, it's hard to see when people do not know Jesus' mission was to reflect the light of the Father's heart. Hence, the martyrs' legacy is a testimony to the magnitude of God's love as experienced in Jesus' words and deeds.

Sadly, many today are caught in a web of misunderstanding and think they have little to say in God's name and leave that to church officials. However, the kingdom does not stand on the rhetoric of humans. It stands on the activities of God's people. To know the heart of God is enough to master the actions of one's soul. As more come to realize God's divine calling, the more the fulfillment of the kingdom, and the "not yet," draws closer to completion.

Throughout biblical history, God attempts to establish a covenant involving the response of humans. God's desire has always been to develop an integral relationship with humanity. And the one ingredient to hold it together is love. However, that is not necessarily the ground conveying within many church precepts and practices.

The chasm correlates to Paul's perception of Jesus' cross as a sacrifice for our sins and has led us astray. According to Paul, by Jesus' action, we are saved from punishment and death. As a result, many today are torn between "good works" and acts of "repentance," while others lean on "faith alone." Although the perceptions may not appear wrong, they are counterproductive no matter the side one may stand on because the kingdom remains on hold and the soul's life is not necessarily set free.

More than his cross, Jesus directs our attention to the kingdom of God at hand. The kingdom has neither left nor is it waiting for us in the afterlife but is here with us! All too many have not understood. In all his words and actions, Jesus' entire life was a testament to the kingdom he proclaimed. And still, the numbers are countless who have not heard. I do not believe this is because people are without ears to hear. Instead, the truth remains hidden while theologians, historians, and others of like mind, debate the question of God's chosen people. Yet, we know all are of God's making!

Jesus says blessed are those who have ears to hear. God's love was then and is now always with us, and so too the kingdom; that is not the question. We are the question!

The Lever of Love

Hurling Stones

I open myself to the Spirit of Jesus and I see objects hurling before me, and then I see an angry crowd throwing stones. I am reminded again of the "Adulteress Woman." He continues:

I Am Light, I Am Love

> Not too many people hurl stones. However, they hurl words, insults, and condemnations much like rocks, some sharp, some blunt, some heavy, and some light. And all have the means to hurt, punish, maim, even to kill. Might I say to kill? And I say 'yes' to kill! Have you looked around lately to see how many are dead in spirit? How many are living unconsciously and emotionally as a wreck? From where does this all come? Ninety-nine percent of it comes from words, harsh language, and insults people hurl every day. I say again. They throw every day!
>
> And do not be fooled. These stones are hurled inside the churches as well as outside the churches. How can you expect a new world when you are so old

when it comes to throwing stones? Oh! You do not realize that or see it because they are not actual stones in your hands. When they threw stones from their hands, be sure, they were hurling words first that poured out from their hearts, and they were not nice words. You know what I am saying.

Through God's voice, God creates the world and its people. Hence, even I, am understood as the 'Word made flesh.' In this sense that I am Jesus the 'Living Word of God,' and in my life, I speak God's words beyond measure. When you read from scripture, do you receive the words I say? When you hear stories in scripture that tell of me speaking words that irritate your soul or rub your feelings the wrong way, I ask you to discern an unfair player's hand. Over time, the scriptures were compromised by writers putting words in my mouth that were not mine.

Words of condemnation skew my message and skew who I am! Then I am taken to the pulpit, and some use those words to rattle my children. I frightened no one! Only some who persecuted me were intimidated by the extent of my courage. In those cases, they were afraid only to see the darkness within themselves.

The vision I give is for the one purpose of assuring you who I am! I am Light, I am *Love*, I am Savior, and I have opened the way for you to follow in my footsteps. My children are scattered, and those who disrupt are like wolves. You may not see them or identify any one of them. However, when you feel your insides rumble, sometimes like seeing a ghost, allow your feelings to be the measure of your hearing.

Many religions teach you less to trust your feelings when, in fact, your feelings are themselves the highest of all measurements for discerning right or wrong in any situation. You must learn to pay attention to them, especially to acknowledge when a stone may hit you because sooner or later, its wound will show up.

What do you do at such times? Straight forward, you sidestep and let the stone pass. It never has to have any effect. When you feel it coming, open your mind's eye, watch it drop into the sea, or fall to the earth. Then turn to the light and let the radiance within show the way.

As a vessel of God's breath, you are a fortress. You are not a victim to anyone hurling stones. You are the victor when realizing, above all else, that you are the son or daughter of God. The Father would never throw a stone at you, nor sanction anyone to do such a thing.

So, can I directly say that feelings are the soul's language?

Many will tell you to deny them. However, when you learn to trust your feelings, you are learning the language of the soul.

Many believe Jesus handed over the "keys" of the kingdom to Peter and the authority to hold peoples' sins bound or let them loose. Such wisdom is not in sync with Jesus Christ. He does not come to judge but to clear a path. He willed not to bind anyone but to set God's people free. The emphasis hails Jesus as Lord over our sins. Jesus is far mightier and with a much higher purpose, presenting himself as lord of the Father's light.

Jesus' power over evil is not the big picture of our Savior but the big picture of our ancestors' perception. In retrospect, he compares God's people with sheep without a shepherd. People were weighed down with heavy burdens with no path forward. God does not desire to hold anyone bound to sin; we do a good job of that ourselves. Such is the story of human history while Jesus tells another story about building God's kingdom.

He is sent to set us free not from sin but to build. Which is more life-giving? Our productivity is God's desire, and, through our God-given free will, we may accept or deny it. To deny is part of a world falling apart. On the other hand, the work of the kingdom is not a heavy burden because it is the pathway Jesus opens into the Father's heart.

The martyrs' empowerment was not because of divine mercy. Instead, through Jesus, they received the Father's love and acceptance. And they were no longer on a bent knee for fear. Instead, they were humbled by God's incredible love that brings them to their knees. God's mystery is less about mercy but genuine love.

Many today inadvertently suppress what they understand as wrong and feel bad. And one might think confessing our sins is a release when more often, it's an expression of our darkness and does not necessarily lead to change because forgiveness is not necessarily an expression of acceptance, especially when confessing the same old sins. Hence, this significantly contributes to the cause of confusion, suppression, and lack of self-esteem among Catholics. However, I am sure the problem is not confined only to Catholicism. Although forgiveness is an act of love, God does not intend that we perpetually weigh in on our faults but weigh in on God's love and acceptance. That is the way to rise!

To listen closely to Jesus' first point of contact with the "adulteress woman" is revelatory. He did not begin with innuendos about repentance; instead, he asked her, "Where are your accusers?" Jesus implied that no one, including himself, was accusing her. Then, what is there to fear? Again, he was not saving her from her sins. Instead, he was quelling her fears and exercising the power of God's love. In that conversation, the light presided over the darkness, and the way of the Son was revealed.

We are a blend of both the dark and the light. The Chinese call this the "Ying and the Yang." This is nothing new. However, the concept discloses a vision for understanding. Jesus focused on the light, not the dark side of the human. This identifies a unique approach in Jesus' wisdom for transforming the lives of those who came to him. His focus on the light is a vital consideration for today.

At times, my regret was overwhelming when I turned to God about wrongdoings, and the hurt I caused to others. I wished I could take it all back, and I cannot. Although forgiven, I sometimes felt like Paul and asked God, "Do you still love me?" Then, to hear God's whisper:

> I never ceased loving you, even if you do not know the depth of my love. Yet, you talk about it but cannot understand with your mind. Do not try to reason with it; open your heart to my love. Believe in my heart, and one day your mind will catch up.

> What makes me any different from Paul?

> At such times, you were not trapped in a sinful nature, but you could have loved more. Hence, the process and pathway into my heart.

Who knows better the disposition of one's soul than the Creator? We are temples of the Holy Spirit. God resides at the heart of each living person. God knows sorrow and repentance, and who can see through fear and confusion better than God? I hardly believe anyone would think they could fool God. And why would they? Of all things, God knows what lies within the human heart, and still, our Maker does not judge. Contrarily, God desires to open a pathway forward.

This approach applies to a good spiritual director whose calling is not to control the life of one's soul to fit specific standards but allows the soul to freely experience God as God presents God's self to the directee. The difference resides in facilitating the relationship as opposed to controlling it. God's love is not concerned with judging behavior but transforming one's soul.

To turn to God with an open heart is to come to him just as you are, and to be assured, the Father will not reject you. You belong to him. He knows your every need, and rejection is not on anyone's list.

Humans are fragile and getting lost in the world's experience can happen overnight. God is far from unaware. We exist in polarity and are held together by "ego." Maintaining balance is not an easy job, especially given the fears that creep their way into our perceptions. Staying in touch with oneself can be a full-time job, eventually, to become a way of being. However, we have learned that believing is about focusing on Jesus.

On the contrary, faith is about staying in touch with the Spirit of God within. Much is written about self-actualization and authentic being, without fear, and the Father's love is the way to prevail and explains how the martyrs endured! Fear is the soul's worst enemy; Jesus liberates us from fear! Hence, reflecting the outcome of his liberating words in the synagogue. And therefore, I emphasized it in the beginning. The visions intend to reclaim your power as a son or daughter of God.

Humankind cannot escape the Creator's love. Such was Jesus' mission to open the eyes of the Father's people. Jesus had a much grander purpose than to save humanity from God's wrath. Do you see how contrary this is to the old perceptions that have been carried through time?

Countless believers do not have a vibrant relationship with God. Here is the tragedy of Jesus' Temple falling. Mostly, they feel they are servants to the Father instead of servants to creation. As such, they share less responsibility for the kingdom and more accountability for paying homage to God. To do so is not wrong, but people are missing the point. The most bountiful tribute to God is service to one another. Do you still see the Temple crumbling or the kingdom coming? God sent his Son so we would see and build on the love that makes us.

Where is Love

No Where

While ruminating about things that keep coming up and haunting me, I engaged in the "vision of nowhere." Naked, I am trapped in a multi-dimensional maze with no escape from side to side or top to bottom. Overhead and beneath my feet, the nightmarish forest surrounds me. The experience is incredibly daunting and an explicit image of being nowhere.

Enclosed by barren limbs and thorny vines they stretch for miles on every side. Feeling the hollowness and fear, I crouch in the unrest of darkness with no way in and no way out.

How did I get here and why? What is this showing me if anything at all? I felt the horror of isolation and helplessness. Jesus did not offer a word. With no resolve, I was left to my thoughts and continued in the haunting of "Nowhere" for three days.

The Prejudice of Men

From where does it come, and is it a real place? Soon I realized that "Nowhere" is the experience of shame and fear. Shame is not the pain for things we did, but for who we believe we are. Jesus was showing me how devastating shame is for the life of the soul. Yes, it's a real place that shackles the spirit within.

"Nowhere" is nightmarish, revealing the desperation that cages the soul and is most difficult to heal. One cannot understand the bewitching void when a soul is trapped and often horrified. And how many cannot escape the oppression plaguing the soul, and worst of all could they ever love themselves again?

The pain is not for things that we have done, but for what is said and done to us. And still many are troubled not knowing where, when, and how shame scuttles them into "Nowhere." They cannot see the enemy, and they know not from where he/she comes, but they know they are in the corners of a maze. At times, it appears they have climbed out, only to find they have not escaped. The darkness overshadows, and again the light dims.

Jesus assures us that shame is not the Father's desire, and "Nowhere" is the work of human hands. The way out is a troublesome road. Yet still, the Father knows hidden secrets, deepest wounds, and the gravest hurts.

Jesus wished not to entrap the Father's children but to set them free, not from God's wrath but from human prejudice. The vision showed me the pains humans suffer and the extent of heaven's sorrow. Indeed, the showing displays how acutely aware the Father and the Son are concerning human suffering. It is frightening to consider the numbers who have committed suicide when caught in the deep dark web of shame and fear.

How many lives have been haunted daily, some since childhood, with no way out? Jesus knows, and the Father knows. "Nowhere" is a desolate place, yet beneath the travesty, Jesus lives. And he calls not just to the one who suffers but for all to see the downfall of love lacking for those who are different, whether by cultural differences, outward appearances, or sexual orientations and God knows whatever more.

Jesus underscores the light of the Father's love. Much like the story about bringing a horse to water. You cannot make the horse drink from it. The same applies to the follower, who Jesus leads not by force or judgment but by one's desire to drink from the Father's cup. It's important to note: God's intention for humanity should not be shaped and judged by the pressure of laws. Jesus was clear about this when responding to the laws and practices during his time. Jesus led the soul in accord with the Father's heart. He said, "...whatever you do to another, you do to me." And today, from our youth, a bracelet prompts us to ask, "What would Jesus do?"

Jesus unveils the Father's heart and through him God's voice. History does not contest the impact of Jesus' words and deeds. How important is it then for our ancestors to hold onto that treasure? Indeed, they are right to do so, however "how" the Church preserves the faith raises an important question about Apostolic Succession.

Jesus opened the way to the Father's heart by reaching into the souls of his followers. He did not transfer his authority by laying on his hands. If there exists any such authority, it is given freely to those striving to duplicate God's heart. Jesus guided his followers with words and deeds that exemplified the Father's heart. History speaks for itself. Jesus revealed that he did not come to be a King. Rather, he was a Shepherd to guide our way. How many see? How many fall to the wayside, especially those lost to the prejudices of men? Who are the heretics and or the persecuted today? Might they be the castaways because they are different in color, sexual orientation, transgender, gay or lesbian, and the list continues?

At this point, how Paul speaks of God's wrath is noteworthy, because if anyone deserved God's rebuke, it was Paul who was killing Jesus' followers. He was not merely insulting them. He was brutally mistreating and sentencing them to death. Left to his own devices, some say Paul might have wiped out the entire Christian community. The point is, Paul did not experience God's wrath. Instead, he revels in God's love and mercy.

I turn to Paul's writings in 1 Corinthians 6, and Romans 1, where he expounds on humanity's guilt. Paul employs God's wrath from the heavens against all ungodliness and wickedness of those that suppress the truth. Yet, he receives God's mercy.

Paul was not merely suppressing the truth but killing the living holy word of Christ in Jesus' followers. I do not know about you, but I would not have let him get as far as he did, and if I were the God he touts, he would not have lived to see another day.

My point runs parallel to a story Jesus told in the Gospel of Matthew, about the unforgiving debtor. He used it to illustrate a fundamental aspect of the kingdom of God. A servant owed his master a grave debt, and when called in to hear what was due, he fell before his master and begged for patience and mercy. In his empathy, the master repealed his full debt.

However, when returning to his affairs, he approached a fellow servant who owed him a much smaller debt. The servant begged for patience and mercy, yet the unforgiving servant had him jailed until his debt was paid. When word got back to the master, he called forth the unforgiving servant and treated him more severely than he treated his debtor.

The point is, the Father does not desire our harsh judgment or wrath. Rather, the Father calls us to be understanding, merciful, and kind as God is merciful, kind, and superseding our measures for understanding. The choices are in our hands. I cannot speak for Paul. I believe he did not know any better. However, that does not make him right, and by now, we should know enough to see through it.

I question whether Paul understood the mercy of God was not only for him. I use this passage because Paul speaks as though from a throne and chastises humanity. I do not know about Paul, but the closer I have come to God, the more humbly I kneel before the Father. And the more respectful I have become to all people. I came to understand that in all who Jesus met, he saw not sinners, but in them, he saw the light of the Father's Spirit. If anything, he invited them into the place of his heart as opposed to rejecting them. God's law is love, and it feeds the human family.

During these times of stress and racial injustice, we are familiar with the slogan, "I can't breathe." I question how much we are also suffocating the life of many devout souls. Indeed, I do not deny that love can be abused, but love is not the abuser. Unfortunately, our ancestors did not make that distinction. What have we to gain by restraining the human spirit with more laws? Are we not able to distinguish what is of God and what is not? Can we make the distinction between love and what is not? If not, can we at least begin to learn? For those who have ears to hear, the ground of the kingdom that Jesus reveals opens the way to be free of fear and free to love.

Paul condemned women with women exchanging natural intercourse for the unnatural. Similarly, he called out men consumed with passion for one another and committing shameless acts with men. He added that they received just penalties for their actions. Whatever that means is not in keeping with Jesus' voice.

Indeed, for many like Paul, seeing from a lesser mindset was common during this early period. Nevertheless, he did not share the perspective of Jesus, who does not judge, condemn, or frighten. Remember, the apostles struggled to understand the teachings of Jesus. I must question then why Paul was decisive about Jesus' mission. Fortunately, many are more understanding today, as exemplified by the cliché, "it does not matter who you love or how you love but that you love."

Many defend Paul's views regarding God's judgment and condemnation, while some water down Paul's aggressions. Here, I recall the effects of Paul's theology as displayed in current headlines. Stories are mounting concerning those gathered outside memorials in protest of gay fallen soldiers. The hate is at once the burial ground of Jesus' kingdom. On the other hand, many say the fall of our country is due to sin. Contrarily, our mess is caused by our lack of love and misunderstanding of the love for which Jesus gave his life.

Why do many believe that God would think so little of people whose love is different? They are the Father's creation. Let me be clear. Many despise what they do not understand and are ready to make judgments. Yet, Jesus expounded on the idea that judging is not of God. How many times did he turn against those who judged others? To be without judgment is a fundamental precept of the kingdom of God!

How many do not understand a man could love another man, or believe a woman loving another woman is heretical? Which is more heretical, to despise them and cast them away or to see through a higher vision? Is there not something more precious beneath the surface that is more important than judgments?

We are astute when it comes to understanding unity within the diversity of cultural differences. However, we tend to be unknowledgeable when it comes to understanding unity within the diversity of human differences. Jesus saw the Spirit of the Father within all who came to him. Jesus' preamble is not aligned with Paul's litany on human nature any more than that of St. Thomas Aquinas. Jesus stood on one solid foundation, and that was, is, and will forever be the solid rock of the Father's love. We forget that each one is an expression of God and if that expression is seeking and expressing love, who dares to throw the first stone?

However, when people judge others who are different, who are they hurting? Who are they judging? Are they not loving? What is there to hate and what are they looking for? Jesus does not categorize anyone or any group by demeaning accusations. He does not call us to judge but to reach more deeply beneath the surface of understanding in and through the Father's love for all of us.

I return to the persecutions over a reign of fifteen hundred years. Each one who died in God's name is yet another broken piece of the Father's heart, whether martyr, heretic, or witch. With each death, God's truth is buried, and the broken pieces shattered further into the dust. We have yet to see through the dust-covered truth of the kingdom Jesus lived and died for that we may build what we are here to create, lest we genuinely fall. As you can see, we are already at the precipice.

Jesus did not close doors but opened them. Who or what gave Paul the authority to overwrite Jesus' truth? Here is the difference between God's kingdom and the laws of men. God is *Love*. Love is not a law. Love is a way of being.

Paul's views came from his limited perception. Today, how many people are outcasts? How many have committed suicide because of the way churches and society treat them? Do you think they are evil? Or did they commit suicide because they were labeled as something they are not? Who knows the mind of God? What would Jesus write in the sand? Yet, we can see the heart of God. Jesus put it on display! And still, many turn to human reasoning. That is where we have been, but not where we need to be.

Jesus' Voice

You have written in a language that is long forgotten, be
not weary that some are unwilling to digest it. However,
be sure for those who have ears, hearts will open.

Here is the Father's Prayer, for those who may be somewhere
in or near the field of "Nowhere."

The Father's Prayer

Take, my children,
My hand
Yes, not my heart
My hand
And I will bury your hand close to my heart
So close that you will feel it beating
I want you to know how loved you are
And how closely I hold you near to me
Be not afraid
Be confident in the home I make of you
You are made not to fall, but
To do great things
Nothing reaches higher than to love
Beginning with yourself

God's Motivation

Scurrying Rescue Truck

Sitting still in the place of prayer, suddenly, my attention shifts to the scene of a rescue vehicle rushing past me. With blazing red lights and a siren piercing the night's shadows, it screeches down the road heralding the life-threatening emergency. Jesus explains:

Peril to the Soul

> The flashing lights signal the need for urgency, and the medics scurry into action. It may be life-threatening or a preventative procedure before the fact. But as you know, emergencies are usually life-threatening situations.
>
> All are fully aware of dangers to the body's life but rarely conscious of fear's threat to the soul's life.
>
> When fear seeps in, the Father and I know how damaging it is to one's soul. Take caution and be affirmed that the Father and I cast out fear. Love is our motivation. The entire vision is to be clear on this single point.

For this reason, I am here to say something is wrong. Wherefore, the Father speaks through the language of tongues, "I paid a great price in the blood of my Son. Why do you still persecute me?" I heard, but I did not understand, until I experienced the injuries myself. When aware, I was bitter and raised my voice against certain precepts and practices of the Church. Although wishing to reconcile with those of the Church I may have offended, making a difference is another story, and it is not easy for me. Often, I wondered if I should have taken a less tempered path. Yet, some say my voice was not loud enough.

I became a priest to proclaim God's love, not his sorrow. However, I cannot deny the extent of hindering the way to the Father. Even asking good and faithful people about their images of God, many if not most, are unsure about God's love for them, all due to underlying fears. Although to be in awe of God is one thing, do you believe when I say the Father desires not our fear? A difference exists between the truth of the heart and that of the head. Do you know Jesus' voice? His sheep do, and they follow! He knows your voice and the fears that hold his voice away from you. Such is not the Father's doing.

I turn to Jesus concerning the speaking in tongues. Paul speaks about the "charism." Many people are confused by this. Some call it hokey while some say, "One shouldn't believe in that stuff." Paul talks about several types of speaking in tongues. Ironically, such is the enigma used to capture my mind and heart.

Jesus' Voice

> Indeed, I understand your purpose. Paul experienced the 'speaking in tongues' in his community and became familiar with the Spirit with them. It kept him in touch

with something more than his traditional understanding. Of course, he could not relate the speaking of tongues to the law or even my cross. However, he knew it was extraordinary. Therefore, to shift his focus to a higher connection with the divine apart from my cross and the law.

So, it was a gift intended not just for the truth of your presence, but for Paul's edification?

First and always, the gifts are for the sake of the community. As you know, Paul was postured to benefit during an extremely challenging period, but still, he did not fully break from his traditional mindset.

More than twenty-five years ago, I experienced "speaking in tongues" on an extraordinary level. Far from contrived, the experience was bewildering. Entirely into the moment, I stood motionless, knowing something incredibly significant was taking place. Since then, I have never forgotten! I remember not only the words but how unforgettable the tone was.

For you that have ears to hear, this is a big deal to God! It is etched in my soul and never left me. Not because it generated fear but because I experienced how deeply God is concerned for his sheep. Proclaiming his sorrow means more to me now than proclaiming his love. Yet, they are intimately tied. I know you cannot have one without the other. And that has weighed on me more than I can express. God wants not your fear but your hearts.

Self-Acceptance

Surfacing Crab

As though peering into a window to see the clear blue sea, I observe a crab slowly floating up to the water's surface. Then, it solemnly folds its legs and closes its claws. The tiny bubbles ripple from its exhale before rushing to the surface. Jesus explains:

Surrender

> The crab rises to the surface just as you perceive. Its arms are closing, or as we see it, coming to rest.
>
> For centuries, in light of their relationship with the Father, my followers were pushed beneath the surface. Some have found different avenues to draw closer to God's love through others of like mind and the rejection of old beliefs. On the other hand, many turn to the churches for their guidance and are pushed underwater. This is primarily due to precepts and practices not aligned with the Father's truth. The pain and sorrow of this grew over centuries. The time is now for rising to human grace and dignity. You are on a mission, and you

are not on a mission to reclaim what you once lost as you understand yourselves as pushed out of the garden.

Rather, my message unveils the garden within your hearts. The paradise discovered in the Spirit of the Father that is already with you. God makes a home in you. No heaven that you can conceive of compares to the paradise of God's presence.

You have been on a long journey, time to rise! Come up to the surface and bring yourselves to rest. If you would, then surrender to the truth and acceptance of self and the Father within. You are a holy creation! The Father and I wish for you to embrace that truth. In the embracing, let go of the darkness and bring yourself to rest.

Jesus teaches us to let go of fear. In matters of spiritual acceptance, let go of fighting everything disturbing the soul! God accepts you as you are at this moment. As you genuinely greet the Father, what you understand as faults and failings do not have to weigh on your heart! Recall the story of the "Adulteress Woman," whom Jesus did not accuse. Instead, he demonstrated love because the Father's love is the essence of life and transformation. The choice is still yours to embrace or deny. It's hard to imagine who would deny this love. However, I wonder how many have not learned of God's love with so much standing in the way. The very reason for the Father's plea and revealing the depth of sorrow in God's heart.

When the Angel Gabriel came to Mary, she was perplexed by his words. Immediately the Archangel responded, "Do not be afraid." And how many times has Jesus said the same to his followers? Chasing away human fear remains a shared message of the Son that has made its way into the biblical narratives. And so, has the precept of the Holy Spirit with us. And here, again, for that reason, Jesus says to his followers, "Do not be afraid; I will always be with you."

The idea of God's dwelling within raises an important question about the order of creation. God spoke, and creation came to order at each sound of his voice. God is *Love*, and with each sound of the Father's voice, love resonated, and light permeated the darkness. By God's nature and design, humankind is imbued also with the love coming through the resonance of God. Put in another way, God is always communicating Godself to us. Books are written about the mystery. God has always and forever loved humanity first.

The Power of Love

A story in Luke 7 draws attention to the power of love. A Pharisee invited Jesus to dinner. While Jesus was sitting at the table, a woman went in to see him. She fell to her knees and began to wash his feet with her tears and anoint them with oil. Those present were appalled. They presupposed that if Jesus is a prophet, he should know the kind of woman she is and not allow her to touch him.

Firing back, Jesus trumpeted the power of love: "She washes my feet with her tears and anoints them with her perfume, and she does not cease kissing my feet. What have you done for me? I tell you that because she loves much, her sins are forgiven. And you who forgive little, love little." Then turning again to the woman, he proclaimed that because of her love, she was forgiven, and later, he added that her love saved her. Jesus, affirmed three times:

- Because the woman loved much, her sins were forgiven.
- The Pharisees loved little, and little was forgiven.
- Her love saved her.

The woman did not defile Jesus, and how difficult it was for the ancient mind to accept the power of a sinner's tears of love and contrition to be enough to free her from sin? On the contrary, as co-creators made in the image of God, all have authority with God to love enough to change the world, let alone transform one's sins.

Jesus was making a highly significant point to those gathered. If anything, Jesus' delivery to them was not about his power to forgive sins but the power of love in every living being. All are made in the image of God. Love's way is central to Jesus' teachings because love is the essence of the kingdom.

The Elders did not understand except only the sin and the need for repentance and retribution. That was the cry of the Old Testament prophets and the direction they understood. Before Jesus, God was feared far more than perceived as a loving Father. To put a face on the Father's love was Jesus' primary objective. By the Father's desire, he eradicates humanity's fear of God, so that the way my open to more productive and life-giving pursuits.

In this case, the woman offered the greatest gift of all, and those at the table did not see it. Their judging nature blocked their way while her loving nature opened her way. Again, it's not the sinner but judging attitudes that defile the heart of the Son and the Father. That is why Jesus asks them, "What have you done for me?" In God's name, they only added to her anxiety. Their prejudicial approach does not align with God's kingdom.

One misses both the eloquence and significance of this entire passage to perceive it any other way. Can you see your love as an ointment and refreshing? If the woman's loving tears were more than enough to anoint Jesus, then why would they not be enough to wash away her perceived sinfulness?

Most conceivably, the Pharisees despised Jesus because he spoke on behalf of a higher court, and just like Paul, they did not understand. When overlaying his traditional perceptions upon the sacrifice of Jesus' cross, Paul saw the Son's truth as easy to configure. Consequently, he taught how Jesus' cross saves us from ourselves.

However, Jesus does not save us from ourselves. Instead, he shows us how to seize our power. I recall the story of the scribe who asked Jesus which is the greatest of the commandments. Jesus replied, "… to love God and your neighbor as you love yourself." "You have spoken well," replied the scribe, to which Jesus responded: "…you are not far from the kingdom of God." Jesus taught that the way of the kingdom is the exercise of love, that is, saving.

In this passage, after demonstrating the power of the woman's love, it's odd that shortly afterward, Jesus repeated, "Your sins are forgiven." In response, the Pharisees exclaimed, "Who is he to forgive sins?" In effect, the scenario is confusing because it switches the narrative to the idea that Jesus is lord over sin. Furthermore, it nullifies Jesus' previous claim concerning the power of the woman's love. I have no doubt this is, yet another misperception configured to align with the teachings of the Old Testament order. Far more than lord over sin, Jesus is the inbreaking of the Father's light intended to illuminate the human heart and soul. Again, "the switch" is most conceivably the author's objective for maintaining continuity with the precepts of Paul.

Jesus! This passage has puzzled me since the first time I read it, and so long ago that I cannot remember. I have not yet turned directly to you to add or subtract your conclusions. My soul aligns, and my confidence in your love has never denied me. However, now I humbly implore your intercession for the sake of those longing for your wisdom.

You speak well, dear messenger. What you demonstrate is the very reason I chose you. You have nothing to fear or to answer to, but only to enjoy the bedrock of love on which you stand. Enough said!

Jesus did not emphasize outward appearances. Nor did he focus on things outside the reach of an open soul. Instead, he delves into the human heart, which becomes the focal point for aligning with the Father's heart.

Jesus publicizes the woman's intimacy with him, which was not at all the elders' shared approach. The temperament of her heart is crucial to Jesus' teachings, while their poor interior dispositions were at the heart of the problem. Still concerned primarily with external appearances, they achieve no insight into satisfying the life of the soul. On the other hand, her intimacy and love for him are transformative.

The more we tend to perfect outward practices, the farther we drift from the soul's life-giving qualities. One need not fear sin, but a house lacking in love.

We have forgotten who made us, from where we came, and who loves us from the day we were born. The question is not about making ourselves perfect in God's sight. Our reasoning and practices do not take us where we ought to be. I am sure you see yourself and where we have landed and the questions looming over us when looking out the window.

Instead, the question is about who we are and why we are here. Jesus came to tell us who we are and why we are here. He sees us not as sinners but as brothers and sisters. We are God's sons and daughters. And Jesus tells us what we are to do.

We have one valuable prayer handed down to us, and it begins, "Thy kingdom come, thy will be done on earth as it is in heaven..."

The prayer demonstrates the gateway into the kingdom that he proclaims. Yet, by the influence of old perceptions, even the sacred prayer is misinterpreted and reverted to a creation focused on sin as opposed to the seat of God's love that was, is, and will always be the focus of Jesus and the Father. Did he, and would he focus on our sinfulness? If he did, how are we to move mountains or do greater things than he? Although we have moved some tall hills and peaks, we have hardly moved a single mountain when up against the course of centuries.

Why would Jesus teach about a place beyond our reach, especially to add that the kingdom is here, now! I do not know which writings were lost, or how, but we have more than enough clues from the past to put the truth into perspective.

Consequently, the first step into the kingdom of God happens when realizing the enormity of the Father's love. This is a challenge, and it's the single reason I am sitting here writing these pages. How tall are the mountains of time and misinformation standing in the way of the Father's love, primarily due to unfound laws written and implemented in God's name? Narrowing the way into Father's heart is intensely challenging to address. However, the plea is first from the Father.

Father, I know the gates do not narrow by your hands but by the work of ancient men that has not unraveled. And the very reason for your plea, "Why do you still persecute me?" What more may be done at this point? I feel we are close to a transition, and so I question.

> Your job is not to change the world, instead to heal the
> hearts of those who have ears to hear. My kingdom does
> not depend on all, although all are invited, not all will

come. Just as written in the parable of my Son when speaking about the 'wedding feast.'

Place of Balance

Retreating Lobster

A corridor opens to me, then leads me beneath the surface of the sea. Jesus opens the door to the action of a lobster clawing its way from a predator! In defense, by the strength of its tail fins, the crustacean backpedals into a small opening between the rocks. Jesus narrates:

The Heart's Realm

> I deliver this image because it depicts the way of life. Every life form from trees to animals and fish of every kind is made with protection mechanisms relevant to their design. Of course, life is a food chain. The Creator understands, and balance is a necessary factor in life. Hence, protection plays a crucial role in the sustainability of God's treasured circle of life. You have the saying, 'eat or be eaten.' And such is the case in the order of life, and not without balancing factors.
>
> In this image, we show you this lobster that swims back to its place of refuge. Because the energies of fear are out of balance, humanity is in a threatened state. As the energies lunge forth, surging like a fiery snake,

knowing where to turn is stressful. Retreat then to the realm of the heart.

Although St. Benedict's rule applies the idea of balancing work, play, study, and prayer, I have not heard much about balance on the soul's level. Numerous books are written, and typically, the spiritual road is about a continuum or a path or ladder hardly anyone can climb. Consequently, many, including our youth, attempt the journey, and after putting forth their best efforts, they give up, and how many feel like failures? Regrettably, the issue is not just an exercise one cannot complete, but the outcomes have consequences that weigh on the soul. Among them is self-reproach for the lack of one's ability to meet a regimen of demands and all for the sake of drawing closer to God.

When one cannot make the journey, it harms the soul's life. The attempts can weaken one's self-esteem and acceptance and add more to the individual's distance from God. Hence, the consequences differ little when seeking to draw closer to God's favor through rules and rigorous demands that one cannot fulfill.

Contrarily, Jesus and the Father illustrate the blending of the human and divine where we stand. That is what this vision captures! God is not testing us but waiting on us to acknowledge the gift we have in him/her. And here reflects the reason for God's plea to the Church because of the laws and practices that often outweigh the rules of divine love and compassion.

I am not saying there is little merit in the strength of spiritual rigors. I am, however, once again, stressing the idea that God's love is first. In my own life, I followed my heart's desire for God, whose love continues to bring me to my knees. Be sure, however, that the road may have its ups and downs, but God's love, from beginning to end, makes it possible and fulfilling. We do not have to prove anything to win God's love, but to each one according to one's gifts, spend God's love on creating a better world. No other gift or prayer to God is more valuable.

What image of God is handed down to so many? What impression did Jesus hand down and is lost? What image of God do you hold in your heart? What greater strength could the martyrs have than faith in an All-Loving and All-Powerful God? "All Loving" does not fit the image of a wrathful God. Jesus illustrates the Father's desire for us to grow in the experience of trusting that God is a good and loving Father. In that, all are within reach of the Father's safekeeping.

We always have had the potential to grow in God's life. However, this is not about being in front of the class or falling behind. That is not God's plan. The Father loves all, and all may know his love according to the degree they are amenable to the Father. Each one serves a purpose, and each one can fulfill and move on to higher degrees within the spectrum of their lives. On the earth's stage, this plays out on varying levels. So, what is going on as I write?

Today, many ask, "Why is there such extensive turmoil in the world?" Although the explanation is not easy to understand, Jesus gave me a story to help draft a picture that may be easier to make some sense.

> He is a young man on his way to school. Because it is his first day in high school, the uncertainty is discomforting. Anxious and reticent, he is unaware of the rules of the road he is traveling. However, eventually, he will find his way, and the tensions will relax.

Like the boy, the world is going through a change. Things are not what they used to be, and we have not learned the rules of the road. God is calling us to a higher standard, and the bar has been raised for humanity. The scope of that higher standard flows through the pages of this book. We are facing more than one road ahead and more than one school to enter. Our choices will determine the road and the door we enter.

Unity in God

Tree with Seven Branches

Coming into view, I see a multi-headed tree displaying an ancestral line sharing the same trunk. Showing seven prominent branches, they branch out to multiply.

The oneness flowing from the trunk reveals humanity's shared origins. Although branching off into many tribes, each branch is its defining heritage. Jesus shows me various tribes multiplying as the branches exponentially divide through the extension of many different sects.

All derive from one trunk, and I see many tribes. The leaves are synonymous with our makeup. We may think differently and have different experiences and perceptions, but we cannot escape sharing one trunk. All are made in the image of God. Jesus attests:

> The Father shows the way not only through the Son but through all creation. The building blocks are in your hands, but hearts are hardening, and the Father's work is not getting done. My quest is to open your hearts and let the work of my hands exercise through your hands.
>
> I approve of human behavior striving for higher goals. Not goals rooted solely in this world, but high standards that reach into God's heart. Must I spell those

tenets out? By design, I would think the human spirit knows the principles from which I speak. Unfortunately, formal training or schooling flowing from the many churches tout various rules typically based on precepts founded on biblical discourse. Although a standard that is credible but not necessarily rooted in my truth.

The New Testament, in its purest form, is not aligned with the Old Testament. Although sharing some truth, the most formidable precepts of my life and purpose are not shared.

The human heart is capable of discerning what is and is not of God more than an ancient text. I do not say this with disrespect for the ancestors but with high regard for their efforts. I acknowledge their process and desire for God. However, that does not make their perceptions my truth. Today, people are stifled and often maimed by the thinking of 'Old,' which rubs against the purity of my heart, and in effect, people believe what is not of me.

Because of the 'Old' influences, New Testament writings are like seeds under rocks. Again, I have no disrespect, especially for the foundational work of the Bible. However, words are skewed over the ages, and they continue to be interpreted in multiple ways and become more divisive as they're channeled through time. Here I point to the ancestors' voices springing from the ground of God's judgment against humans.

Open your heart and listen well. What comes from the Father also comes from me, and we do not divide. We do not lash out against our enemies with hate or judgment. However, we nudge in loving ways to sway you, although never to force a change of heart. Instead, we desire to assist God's children to see with an open heart.

Jesus demonstrates the wisdom within the human heart we often fail to exercise, yet the inspiration flows from the core of what it means to be made in the image of God. The attributes of love define a common ground for races and creeds, yet our intellects divide us.

Many believe they are inadequate when attempting to initiate a relationship with God. The intention of Jesus' mission is revealed when placed against the foil of a disturbing history. God is not the one who divides, nor Jesus who defines the heretics. Instead, steeped in fear and heartlessness, the divisions among men and women are from our hands. Hence, Jesus delivers the vision of the one trunk with seven branches that are not united.

The Father's Voice

Unity is found only in and through me. I am the ground of unity.

What is the message of this vision? Is it humanity's divisions, lack of harmony, and the inability to affect better and stronger relations?

The purpose of this vision is to raise awareness of humanity's challenges and failures. Humanities' course started long ago. Can you not see the crowds my Son gathered? Can you not see what is possible? Indeed, the Church faltered. It caused more division. The 'One

Trunk' is not merely about many cultures but untold systems of belief. However, if you look around the globe, most are reaching for the sacred.

However, some are severed from the 'One Trunk,' and they do not seek the truth, rather their selfish pursuits. By now, the differences ought to be clear between those seeking the sacred and those who are not. What might you conclude when viewing from this perspective? Already, you are processing the possibilities.

So, am I right to think of the possibility for humanity to converge on a different level, wherefore those seeking the highest good may strengthen when uniting. Here, for the sake of world peace. However, my question is: Has the approach been tried before?

Not as you think!

Beyond Wings

Flight of the Eagle

Overshadowed by the heights of the canyon, I see the eagle soaring effortlessly under the hot sun. Circling through the blue skies, the majestic bird grows smaller as it rises beyond the rocky peaks, then fades into the clouds. Jesus continues:

Standing in Our Own Way

Flying the highest of all birds, they can see their prey below with the sharpest eyes at exceeding distances. You know the expression 'eyes of an eagle.' Hereto, they have the gifts necessary for their survival as with each species for good reason. Prominent birds, they are the well-respected emblem of American strength and ingenuity. Proudly, they display on your currency, but what about this eagle that I show you? Is it too flaunt because it looks bold and refreshing to exhibit, or do you see the weightier message beneath the vision?

The point I make concerns another side of the eagle that flies so high. From the vantage point of humans, the eagle is a flawless creature. Having everything it needs: powerful and sharp talons; a daunting wingspan; and a sharp beak used of course to pierce and eat its prey. The eagle falls short of nothing, but there is something about the eagle that no one sees. The eagle soars high into the sky but it is bound to the earth's pull. So, even in what you understand to be free as a bird comes with limitations.

In humanity's exploration and expansion of its technological realm, humanity is losing sight of its limitations. Humans dare to defy their ability in space travel. You have not mastered the exact sciences for such an endeavor. Yet, you spend excessive amounts of time, effort, and funding for so little in return. And, with little promise of success, you continue with this game.

And so, the question that I raise: Is this honestly for the greater good? If you spent as much time, effort, and money on cures for illnesses and peace in the world, you would have gained far more success.

However, underlying fear is prevalent. And that is why you are limited. Unfortunately, fear has pushed you toward an attitude of dominance.

The conflict has continued since the beginning of time. One region against another; one kingdom against another; one state against another; one country against another; one nation against another; and the aggression has not stopped. With all your intelligence and abilities, you enforce rules to dominate. Who dares to apply ideas to affect peace?

Oh! You think stability is not achievable because of those who see and think differently. Yet, which is more challenging to advance, dominance, or peace?

Where has fighting got anyone? A lesson that's not learned even to this day. Threatening war without considering the consequences makes dominance an evil game.

Imbalance and disruption are products of domination. They go full bore against the grain of the kingdom to which I focused. I pointed out the crucial act of service to one another. As I am of service to you, so also you must be of service to one another.

But your eyes are still closed with little time left. Eyes must open now. Otherwise, the world that you are creating will be destroyed and not by my hands. But by those who seek stability without the insight to gather people. Contrary to what you are hoping for, you will destroy one another.

You say you want peace. I know this is true and what you desire in the deeper recesses of your hearts. However, how can you want peace and turn to violence to achieve it? A lesson you still have not learned. So, in your fear and dominance, you continue. When humanity understands that domination is not the answer, you may make progress in peace and stability.

The message speaks for itself. May I add a mega issue before us? So, I ask you, Jesus, what do we do, those of us who have no voice in world decisions for war or peace? Are we only to pray? Is there anything more? Most people around the globe wish for peace, but world leaders seek other agendas. What do you expect that we, the people, can do?

You ask an important question. I know what you are saying and what you are thinking about prayer. I am going to give you more than another prayer. I am going to provide you with a picture of what you can do. Each one carries the weight of God in their hearts:

- Can you gather in numbers, not necessarily in buildings but in mind and heart?
- Do you believe God will listen?
- Do you believe in your desire for the greater good?
- Do you believe your heart is sincere about God's message to build a better world?

In your heart, picture the world you seek, and that will be your most powerful means to achieve the outcome for which you hope. However, the landscape you portray is not about painting and walking away from it but putting yourself into the picture every day until the portrayal is your everyday. Powerful are the numbers when gathering in heart, mind, and spirit.

Does that mean embodying the vision and then sharing its light by living in its light?

The exercise is about the power of manifesting your truth when aligning with God's truth.

Sounds too simple when facing the mess of a complicated world?

Of course, your response is understandable. I do not wish to oversimplify; however, creation is not necessarily so complex. The complexity concerns the use of free will. I am suggesting an answer according to the productive use of human free will in conjunction with trust in God's intentions for creation.

In this case, I feel the desperation much like the Old Testament ancestors waiting on a Messiah.

The ground of the Father's heart is not a desperate place, but the only place to turn. From there, you may find your answers.

We are in a divide. My heart weeps for those who love and indeed seek what God desires for the world. However, it appears we are losing to adversaries that do not align with your love and instead seek to dominate. Although I cannot see what you see, I am not afraid, for I know the depths of your love. However, I do not like what I see, and that is incredibly challenging. The indifference does not appear fair to me and indeed not acceptable.

The Father Responds

You are not alone, and for those who hear and understand this line of communication, I say this: I Am the Creator of all, including both sides, and for reasons that you do not see. I do not wish violence or harm, and those who use such measures will not dominate. How often stated in the pages of this book that 'love is the most powerful force in the universe?'

Father, I wish not to be divisive. Although the Church is slow to move, the Pope has many honorable leaders with him, and many are kind and loving, but there is a need for change. I have heard it said from within and outside its walls. I know many efforts are intended for the greater good, such as schools, hospitals, and goodwill on many levels. Credit for the genuine work must be honored. I know you are not without eyes to see what I say. I wish for your perspective while knowing your view is more valuable than mine.

Thank you for being so kind to understand this is not about division nor judgment, right or wrong. Sometimes, the task is hard for humans to express both sides of a situation. So, let me say what needs to be said.

When saying the Church has failed does not mean a complete failure. However, problems linger, and they need addressing. Yes, I am calling for changes, and they are significant. Time is running out. Hence, the heightened intensity of our dialogue.

Be sure I know where there is love and where there is not, and those of my heart's purpose, I will not deny. And there are many to be grateful for, and they know who they are. This work does not intend to offend anyone but those who may not understand. A change is coming, and I want all to be a part of the highest and best outcomes. I do not condemn anyone. That is not my way. Hence, my words are vital because they are not about what I am doing to you but what you do to one another.

The "Tree with Seven Branches" suggests the possibility for humanity to converge on a different level for affecting peace. I questioned if the idea was a rerun, and you responded, "Not as I may think." I have listened, and now Jesus adds, "The ground of the Father's heart is not a desperate place, but the only place to turn."

When seeing the ideas side by side, I understand your intentions. You are saying that your will is not about a single body of believers, denomination, or sect of any kind crying out or alone. Instead, your will includes the voices of all people in awe of your majesty, no matter the creed or not – all joining in one mind, body, and spirit with one cause in God's name, no matter how your name is said or understood, but that you are the one trunk to a severed family.

> You are speaking on behalf of the vision Jesus proclaimed.

Jesus left us an everlasting impression, and he says we will do "greater things than he." Now is the time for us to leave a lasting impression on God's heart. I believe in the people around the globe and the one God of all Creation. And that the kingdom Jesus proclaimed was not about a chosen sect, denomination, or religion but all blessed men and women "with ears to hear" and aspire to the truth of God's intention for the human family. The time is near, and the hand of God will change the course of humankind as we unite heart, mind, and spirit to reclaim the one foundation of all creation.

> I will change the course of human history for those with eyes to see and ears to hear. My promise is to gather my children in love.

Father, the profundity of your words makes me think how we have lost the truth of your desire because of the extended focus on sin and restitution. Jesus declares your favor is with us, now! Once again, you seek to be heard, not for judgment but love. Although it weighs on me that you would choose me to reclaim your favor. I feel like a lonely voice in the wilderness that cannot hide from the intensity of your love, not your will. Therefore, I persist.

Because of your undying persistence to love and be loved, your intent hallows my being, and I hear your voice from twenty-six hundred years, "You shall be my people, and I will be your God" (Jer 30:22).

> You have written well the exposition of my heart, open
> to those who seek my heart and nothing less.

Although Jesus repeatedly taught with words, examples, and deeds, many do not engage the love of God as a two-way street. What are they misunderstanding?

> The question is not necessarily a misunderstanding but
> running astray.

Do you mean surpassing the boundaries of your heart?

> I mean falling short of the boundaries, and sometimes
> so short, I have seen hell and not what I have created, a
> vision of humanity's design, and I weep not in anger but
> with a heart that bleeds.

I have no words to utter, only to humbly bow before you, not for mercy, but in awe!

> I want you to rise from your knees and speak my truth
> that will be enough.

PART 4

Where We Should Be

Ground of God's Love

Thief in the Night

Quaking Earth

As I view the earth's shaking, I witness a devastating panorama. Unimaginable to behold, I am startled by the earth's rupture and the width, breadth, and depth of destruction in its aftermath. The ground is an opening wound. I stand back! Jesus explains:

Art of Creation

> In some regions of the world, people are familiar with the devastations of earthquakes. The traumatic awareness is gripping when looking into the depth of a chasm that did not exist a day ago. To see it is frightening. Many say the tragedy is not by God's accord but by the nature of science. Yes, that is true, although God is at once also the Father of science. So often, it begs the question, or at least, for some explanation since the earth is by God's design. God made it perfectly as it exists. Science, as I see it, is humanity attempting to understand the God event.
>
> What I mean is the earth is not static, but rather dynamic, i.e., a place within the universe that is eventful, organic, alive, and mobile. You know it spins on an extraordinary axis, and science is beginning to

see, more inexplicably, the earth's movement through the galaxy. Your planet is an event, continually happening. Although God can affect any circumstances, creation is set into motion and is perfect in function, design, and purpose precisely as it exists. God does not interfere with the processes of life and death.

Hence, I make the point: Questions arise concerning things as dramatic as an earthquake would come from God's hand. The incident is a part of the living, dynamic functioning of the earth not meant to frighten humanity. To question is not about who, but rather, what.

God does not hurt humans. On the contrary, God reconciles the travesties that occasion your human experiences. In the Father's eyes, nothing gets lost. Remember, God is eternal, and God made you in God's image. The Father of life will utilize the tragedies for delivering a higher good. You have not learned yet, the full hand of God in all things as they exist. Be sure there are no victims.

The planet's functioning and our place on the globe are far beyond what the eyes can see. Remarkably, the earth is a harbinger of life and mysteriously orchestrated to a fitting purpose. God's masterful vessel is vibrating to a perfect balance beginning with its point of axis and spinning the seas safely over its surface while gently wooing the lava within its womb. From the Creator's hands flow mysteries beyond what the eyes can acknowledge, although to see God's breath and beauty in every corner.

As glorious as it sounds, how do we respond when jolted by its unpredictable nature? Although framed in a new way, it is an age-old question, and God's answer does not change. Perhaps people of the world are not listening. God is often to blame and misunderstood when the earth and its moodiness clash with humans, and the results are tragic. Beyond the grasp of the mind, the earth is a remarkable feat. What would life look like if not for creation's beauty and dynamic nature?

Adapting to the earth's changes, animals exemplify some savvy. Humans have a different approach. Many are simply stubborn or in fear of change, and they deal with the looming threats. How many know they live in an environmentally dangerous area? Yet, they return and rebuild only to await the next disaster. The phenomenon is interesting, even for the Father who protects and warns. However, he does not tell people what they should or should not do.

Some regions come with their known scientific downfalls, and that should be enough to either build appropriately or settle in another location. God does not put people in harm's way. Rather, given the parameters of each situation, he watches over them. The Father cannot reshape the globe to conform to the choices of men and women. To do so would eventually throw the entire balance of creation into another spin.

With all its difficulties, the earth is precisely according to God's intentions for serving a grand purpose. We cannot know God's mind, but trust in the *Love* that makes us, even in the face of calamity. The point underscores the martyrs' legacy.

During these troubling times, we are facing an unprecedented pandemic. I turn to the Father for help to understand. I feel the uncertainty of Jesus' words about the time that will come like a thief in the night without warning.

The Father's Message

Of course, this is an extraordinary event on the planet. I can assure you that I am not the 'thief in the night.' On the contrary, you are experiencing the plague of your undoing. Do you see the power of free will? You may ask, what did I do? Wherefore the consciousness of all is collectively affecting the whole, and it must change. Understand the precepts of the kingdom my Son proclaimed and choose accordingly.

I do not have to talk about the ethos of individualism, though it is counterproductive to the proclamation of my Son. You know the ideology. Sadly, you also have churches that talk about the Body of Christ, then shred it with laws and rules that divide and judgments that maim the soul's life. There is enough blame to go around. If that is what is coming out of the Father's house, what things might you expect from that which is not of the Father's house?

Yes, there is a fork in the road, for you who have ears to hear, know the path to follow. Although some may believe to see an end to the turmoil, I say only the beginning. Now is the time to choose your direction. The garden exists within. Understand that I am the treasure, and how you spend or deny is in your hands.

My Son spoke about talents. If ever there was a time, now is to use them wisely. Far less than a thief in the night, I tell you not to be in fear. Instead, from the innermost depths of my heart, awaken to my Spirit with you!

Father, I know you do not instill fear in your people. How is it that the disruption may continue?

I am not against humanity, and if I were, I would not be adamant about the inception of this book. Now hear me. I do not will for anyone to be left behind.

My will is for my children to understand that I am with you. But I cannot accept those who refuse to act according to the nature of my heart. Let that be your guiding light. I love you and wish you to love as I love you. Love does not work from fear. Find your peace in me and know you will find your way through me.

Divine Majesty

Sovereign Pyramid

Jesus whisks me into the horizon of another time. Awestruck, I stand before a towering pyramid. Trimmed by majestic trees caressing its enormous base, the panoramic view is hypnotizing. Looming overhead like a mountain stretching across the terrain, the pyramid extends incredibly into the sky. So much I wished to absorb, but I could not escape the gaze of the surreal Egyptian Sphinx looking down on me. Masterfully yoked to the body of the monstrous lion, the mythical sculpture radiates forbidding vibes. Jesus reveals:

God's Magnificence

> The Egyptian goddess with a beautiful headdress personifies a commanding mind and intimidating strength, an icon of intelligence and power. She displays not an untamed might but a winning balance of beauty and intelligence.
>
> The immensity of power conveyed in the Egyptian goddess is a signpost to anyone who would dare enter or draw near the pyramid. She exhibits the sacredness

and the awe of the pyramid. Yet, its total projection is not near the immensity of the Creator's dominion.

Far less than a signpost of omnipotence that gives warning to one's approach, nothing is more magnificent than the one God of all creation. Here, not because of God's might, but that the Father of all draws near. Unbelievably, the Creator makes a home within each one. However, each one must awaken to God's Spirit!

Jesus, you saw the Father's light in all you encountered. That is why you were kind, even to your enemies. Why is it that we still do not see what you see?

Although eyes begin to open, the expectation is not probable for most. Indeed, creation is an ongoing process. Have we not come to the end of our time? Are we not held back by the reigns of limited understanding?

Have we misunderstood how intimately tied we are to the Father? What will it take to open the eyes of God's people so that they may see more clearly the Spirit of the Father in others? Most omnipotent God, and awesomely gentle Father who makes a home of his children. What more is there to love and to worship? Who is to fear? Love is the most powerful force in all creation. You are the ground on which to stand and move mountains!

How limiting the perception when believing God is waiting on us to be worthy, as opposed to God already with us? It's also limiting to believe that God is distant, yet God is in our midst. God with us is the kingdom of God to realize, but not yet complete, hinging on the seeing of men and women.

Although, in all sincerity, something most profound exists in the analogy of the Sphinx's dominion when considering how the eternal God resides in the fragile human. Indeed, dear Jesus, this is hard for the mind to grasp.

> You must let go of the rational mind and enter the holy place of your heart, for there exists the indwelling of God, a mighty place. However, you see yourselves as small and fragile in God's eyes. Yet not only are you made in God's image, but you are the living pyramid of his presence. When you see this, you will begin to understand the peace, strength, and inner beauty of all you are meant to be.

Father, I was one growing up who saw myself unworthy in your eyes. On the day, I asked, "How do you see me?" I would never have conceived your perception of me; to ask was trying. And after the intense pause, you responded, "I love you. You are my son." And that was a "game changer" for me. And it was a game changer for who I wished to be. Yet, I have been on a long journey for over thirty-four years, and I have caused little to change in your name.

Well, that is about to change.

If people only know what I know about you, since that day, that has been my wish! Father, could you… a prayer for those who are feeling as I once felt?

The Father's Table

Sit at table with me
I have time for you
I love you

Do not be afraid
My desire is for your love
Not your fear

Be not afraid of who you are
You are my son, my daughter
And you are made perfectly in my image

Sit with me
Rest your head upon my shoulder and,
Find comfort in me

Nature of God

The Gingerbread

I see a turkey in the backdrop of an autumn harvest spreading its captivating wings. When suddenly, as though riding on a pinwheel, my thoughts cascade into the autumn leaves and the holidays only a few steps away. Then aroused by the delicious image of gingerbread, I could not deny its plump size and shape. Swiftly, my surroundings shift to the heart of all holidays and Christmas Day draws nearer. To see how delicious and rich I could almost smell and taste it! Jesus narrates:

Beloved Father

> Gingerbread is a hallmark of Christmas, a season of joy and celebration, and how I come to you. The gingerbread is a metaphor for the Bread of Life that I am. I give of myself, not just to sustain but also to enhance human potential. The offering of the Father's love, among all things, comes with many blessings of joy, peace, and glad tidings. Life's finest spices come from the Father. Is that not my reading from the scriptures as proclaimed in the Synagogue? Henceforth

is the peace in which I come in the Father's name and the Father's joy and celebration!

Nothing is more potent than the blessings I bring, all in the Father's name, to bring joy to the soul. For you to see that as I am friendly and kind, so is the Father gentle and caring. As you know, Elders of the Synagogue were not so kind. They placed heavy burdens on people intending to hold them to their authority, denying their flock empowerment and God's acceptance. In truth, there began a resurgence of such power the day the Church took root in my name.

I do not put you through hoops. I give you the depth of the Father's love that you will stand in that light and become yourself the light. You live in the Father's heart not through mortification, not through retribution, not through penance and absolution, but only to draw near to him with an open heart. In that light, you are made clean. Through your willfulness, embrace him. Anyone wishing to come into his light, he will not turn away!

Jesus shines a light on the genuine nature of the Father's heart. What more to be thankful and joyful than the gift of the Father's love, and the Son who reveals it? The apostles had difficulty understanding where Jesus was taking them. It's interesting to note that today, many do not understand why they struggled. Instead, most believe that we have faith and church down to a near science. How many go to church and then return to everyday life? They are comfortable knowing the rules and regulations.

Consider that Jesus points to two fundamental precepts that create the church. They are the love of God and love of one another.

Far more than going to church, they lead the way for becoming Jesus' Church/Temple. Jesus fostered an attitude toward life that flowed from the inner spirit of the heart.

A path for being in the Spirit of God encourages kindness and compassion. Eyes are wide open to the elevated challenges we face in today's world. Jesus said, "... we will do greater things than he," and now is no time to kick that under the rug but to see through the eyes of the heart!

Humanity has created an ethos about God, who is barely reachable. God is often portrayed as a judge whose perception is like humans. Consequently, many feel they should avoid God. How hard is it for them to experience and accept that God is a kind and loving Father? Understanding God's nature is the crux of the difficulty then overlaid by the duality in which we live. Of course, embracing our Creator is challenging, but for a good reason - and reason enough for the Son to bring God's heart to life.

As understood, Jesus was the incarnate comingling of the human and the divine. Lest we forget we are made in God's image, and we also share in the comingling of the human and divine. However, most are unable to accept themselves as such. And do you know why?

For the most part, many consider themselves fallen since the beginning. Interestingly, we also believe we are temples of the Father's Holy Spirit, although Paul puts an ancestral spin on the idea. The apostle proclaimed that we are temples of the Holy Spirit, but he uses the platitude to press on us instead of lifting us (1 Cor 6:19-20). Consequently, faithful people hear more about the problem of sin and are propelled by an urgency, as though God is looking over their shoulders as opposed to a life-giving and loving presence.

Could Paul's reasoning be why so many approach God feeling that they owe God something? I am not saying we have nothing for which to be thankful. On the contrary, we have more reason to be grateful when aware of who we are because of who God is to us. The act of creation is far more than gratuitous. To be made in God's image is a holy action flowing from God's heart who makes us on purpose for a purpose. To owe God our love is not loving at all. Love cannot be owed and be love. Love is a way of being that flows through humans, not to owe but to complete the image in which we are made. Indeed, we are temples of the Holy Spirit.

However, because Paul defaults to Old Testament systems of belief, he emphasizes incompetent human nature, sin, and due punishment. Again, Jesus teaches the kingdom of God for which we are made not simply to survive but to flourish, but how many have understood?

Despite our weaknesses, we find more strength when focusing on God's light instead of the perceived darkness. The Father does not bind anyone up with doubts and fears. God's desire is for our love, not our homage and repentance. To love one another is our cardinal act of worship, not to owe, but to love by living on the ground of the Father's heart laid down for us through the life and death of the Son. Recall that Jesus never failed to love. Forgiveness was an aspect of his love and hardly the full measure of his cross.

As a child, I remember being told that we are temples of the Holy Spirit. I sat up and lit up! Until the supposed blessing came with instructions and mandates about behaving in every way. It came to the point that the Spirit was something to be feared. How many feel they are in debt to God? I have witnessed how poorly people perceive themselves, less as spiritual and more as outcastes. Hence, this is a residue of old teachings that still haunt many of today's churches, and again, cause for the Father's plea.

To see beyond the existing ideals is near impossible when facing a Church, the size and breadth of centuries. Unfortunately, many are complacent and do not look further into the truth of their dignity and strength in God – not enough passes on from the pulpits that build on human nature from this light. Yet, God's living Spirit is with and within all, and few are taught the meaning. Sadly, believers perceive the "mystery of the Spirit" is for special advocates to explore. To some degree, which is true, but what defines the advocate is the question.

To define such a soul is not a long stretch. Jesus teaches the love of the Father. The advocate's way begins with the intention to approach the Father with an open and sincere heart so that one's soul may awaken. That is the first step.

Unfortunately, Paul does not have Jesus' wisdom to comprehend what it means to love as God loves or the understanding to live in the reflection of God who makes us. Instead, he lays his burden on Jesus' cross. We are far more than static beings waiting on God. On the contrary, God is waiting on us to build a kingdom that is "not yet complete" though empowered by the ground of God's love.

Instead, most venture into paths to overcome the darkness, and the road is a daunting climb. Of course, to love as God loves is a mighty feat, though ironically, a path less burdensome than a war against sin. Here is the troublesome core many do not understand and the sole reason that makes Jesus different than any other man. Under the most challenging circumstances, Jesus never failed to love. Where would we be today if he did? Although Paul confuses with assumptions about God and Jesus' mission to free humanity from sin, we have learned more about paying homage to God than the necessity of our love for transforming the human family. Our mission is to share in Jesus' holy life and the love of the Father he revealed. Although Jesus' love made it through, our posturing is not necessarily on solid ground.

Because love is the answer to our transformation and being, the kingdom is not progressing as God intended. Again, Paul does not have Jesus' wisdom to comprehend the depth of what it means to love or the ability to live in the reflection of God who makes us.

Here again, on different levels, whether subtle, explicit, taught, or experiential, many feel how the emphasis on sin trumps our ability to love. Jesus did not teach a spiritual way by pressing against sin. Jesus opens the way to a loving Father. Here, God's love is our motivation, and our progress is achievable. Jesus calls us to walk in the light of the Father's love, whereas love is the focus. To be sure, the way is challenging, although achievable, and never diminishes the soul's life.

Ground of God's Love

Cresting Ocean Wave

I am given the breathtaking vision of an enormous ocean wave cresting beneath the golden sunlight's illuminating rays and cutting through its peak. Vibrant and refreshing, the crashing wave washes onto the shore. Jesus reveals:

Breath of God

> When believing the proximity of God's breath, one may ride upon a crest that carries the soul above all concerns. Much like sailing atop a wave with a clear view of the horizon as you move forward through life. And when there are dips and turns, you learn as a baby to crawl and then to stand and then to walk. You gain assurance that you are always safe riding the winds of God's breath.

When it comes to knowing the depth of God's love and where God may carry you, Jesus points to the image of a child learning to stand and destined to walk, to run, and to grow tall. The invitation here is to trust that we are not fallen people who need to wrestle our way past our sins. Instead, like the martyrs, we are meant to rise as Jesus rises in the Father's love. Jesus came above all to breathe the

Father's Spirit into this world. To see it any other way is to deny Jesus the gift of the Father's love for which he laid down his life.

Jesus, is that not the story of humankind: A series of fallings; a series of getting up only to fall again? Why tell us something we have known for so long?

Dear child
You have not known
My message has not reached your heart
My message has been circumvented
Like water to fall upon a garden
And swept away by the wind
You have been told that your nature is to fall
And that you can get up in Jesus' name
I tell you that your nature is not to fall
Your nature is to rise
Your nature is to build
You were never fallen
The Father lives in you and through you
You are here to build
You have forgotten

I recall the story of a weeping child. After a church service, a young mother approached me with her child one Sunday morning. She was still in Pre-K. The mother greeted me with concern and then explained that her child asked her a question she could not answer. She decided to see me after the service that day so that her daughter could pose the question. Stooping down to peer into her soft teary eyes, I could hardly see them. Looking to the ground while rubbing her eyes, she spoke with a heartsick voice that I have never heard from a child. Hesitantly, she asked, "If I die and go to heaven and ask God to send me back to mommy, would he say yes?"

Of course, my heart was weeping with her. I immediately said to her, Catherine, I do not doubt that if you ask God to send you back to mommy, he could not help but say "yes"!

Some may disagree, but here is the distinction between the intellect and the Father's heart. What benefit is there in telling the child something she is not ready to understand and would only cause more fear and harm to her soul? Some rely more on books than what lies within the heart of God. Perhaps, an example of the "dark ages" and the "torch of terror" is simmering still.

I think about one so young, and thankfully, knowing the Father's heart, I may not have placed her on an ocean wave but safely in a boat to sail the wind of God's breath. Indeed, I chased away her fear, and she was already safe in God's care. Such is what it means to be God's hands and voice in the world. Are we not to realize the truth in this? Jesus' every action and every word were reflections of the kingdom and drawing near with love. We are all called to be the word and works of God's living truth. The more we know of the Father's heart, the more we rise with Christ, and the kingdom comes.

The Father's Voice

> For one so young, her heart sweeps me into the glory of creation. The love she has for life and her mommy fills my heart beyond the measure of worship. She reflects the precious gift I give and why I give the gift of my Son.

Your words come with overwhelming gratitude. They reflect the gift of life and love for which your Son came. Primarily, to chase away our fears.

A Prayer to Start the Day

> May I see with the eyes of the Father's heart
> May I listen with the ears of the Father's heart
> May I speak with the wisdom of the Father's heart

When God is First

Rocket Launch

I was preparing for the vision Jesus was about to show me because he gave me the sense of its powerful nature. After a single breath, the view opens to a bright blue sky, and my seeing fixes on a rocket about to launch from its docking pad. Before my next breath, the fire blasting from its ports overshadows the dock in heavy clouds of smoke. Propelling the colossal ship straight up into the atmosphere, I see only the fire burning in the sky. Jesus begins:

God's Intention

> Modern science and technology, through God's eyes, are primitive. However, what is miraculous about science and technology is the unfolding of the intelligence of humankind. Manipulating matter through science, humanity continues to develop remarkable crafts.
>
> Nevertheless, in the bigger picture of intention for their use, they are very primitive. Humankind is in the infancy of its technological heights, but there is more to this than meets the eyes. In the making of such vessels and the development of space technology, the designers become like horses with blinders. They see themselves

as uniquely intelligent and specialized in the way they manufacture and develop their products. Indeed, the spacecraft's construction is exceptional, and so too are the satellites set into motion. Although accomplished when considering space travel, you are still light years away from becoming masterful. If you continue with the same intent for the technologies that you are using, you will continue to be inefficient.

Pure science is the study of physics, yet few delve more deeply into physics when it comes to technological advances. Here, simply because all things are of God and from God. Because God is Prime Creator, is God not the most authoritative physicist long before any human? The Father is an infinite being, whereas the human is not. An extreme void exists between God and human intelligence.

Here is my point, most who delve into the sciences skip one fundamental component: God! The lack of attention is quite a shame! They do not know how to access Godly heights through God, so they struggle with limited means.

God has many means for humanity to reach heights for change and development. Humankind is not necessarily grounded; any more than the kingdom of God is someplace up in the skies that you must reach up to it. If humans would see things a little differently in their explorations, the first question they ought to ask is, what is the purpose in this? Where is it to take us, and how will it serve humankind?

For the most part, space technology advances are attempts to dominate one country over another. And so, the motivation is to pull ahead. More often, the reason is fear. Think about that for a moment in your developmental sciences, especially regarding space travel.

Suppose the underlying motivation was a love-based approach and therefore aligned with the Father's design for humanity, i.e., to be in service to each other. In that case, there could have been more advancements when considering the most crucial aspect that God is the Creator of space and all things therein. My question is, where are you going with that?

You direct your energies more from fear and destruction. You are choosing from the darkness, which does not excel your progress. Instead, transcend your abilities by taking the essential components and putting them first.

Jesus is speaking on a scientific and technological level only to make a point about aligning with God's intentions. The effort is relevant to the entire human project. When our objectives run contrary to the Creator's, where is the power? On the other hand, when aligning with the Father's design, humanity can reach exceptional heights. You may find that such travel is not only achievable but with less difficulty.

While looking back to the years leading into 2020 and beyond, one sees the turmoil upon the earth. God is watching, and it's time for humanity to decide. Will we continue in our own often broken and inapt ways, or will understanding shift our priorities? Jesus speaks to scientific and technological developments and every aspect of human development from politics, religion, industry, economics, ecology, and everyday life.

Some may say, "Listen to this; it seems that God does not know God's creation." God knows God's creation and the advance is in our hands. All is for a reason, and all is well. In our thinking, we will not see it. Only through the eyes of the heart, awareness comes. God knows his people, especially the language of their souls. The Father is aware that not everyone will see, but many will, and in them, the kingdom comes.

When viewing the study of physics, Jesus sees what is lacking in the development of spacecraft. Of course, one might think that physics and technology work hand in hand. They do, but not as one might think. The study of physics is developed for getting to the bottom of how things work. Well, then look at it this way: God is at the forefront of how everything works and is often left out of the equation!

Our God-given world overflows with a myriad of potentials and possibilities. Presenting us with a single lens we must not ignore. Jesus renders insight for achieving humanity's most benevolent outcomes for a safe and prosperous planet. However, if fear stands between us and our highest potential, we will not succeed.

Can you see why the Father would send the Son to quell our anxieties? We are not here to escape a fallen world but to build a new world. Our greatest enemy is fear, and if that is the engine that drives us, indeed, we may end up exactly where we wish not to be.

Father, I do not deny the fear factor, but where is the stumbling block for humanity when aligning with God's intentions, or as I often say, the order of creation?

> Perhaps in another book, however, the question is raised, and I will give you a peek into the problem. Humanity's growth is impeded by many who pressure it with the force of fear and added destruction. My Son's

ambition was to lift the fear, and as you can see, he succeeded, but his legacy did not, as the story now reveals.

So, the more significant stumbling block is not humanity's ability to find strength in me, but the lack of truth and belief in themselves. If you could see in yourselves what I see, the planet could transform overnight.

Have you not given us eyes to see and ears to hear?

Again, perhaps in another book to write, although I will give you a hint called the gift of free will. In it, you have the power to choose what you see and what you hear.

Navigating the Pains of Life

Jesus' Face is Charred

Misty shades of darkness rush into every corner of my room. I feel its chill passing through me. From above, a dim light is pointing downward, displaying his tomb. On top rests the crushing slab sealing it shut, then to see it lifting my soul recoils. His face is charred, as though burned by fire and smoke. Less than glorious, the vision of Jesus opening the tomb from within is haunting.

Undoubtedly, this is not the resurrection of Christ, as we understand. Instead, he appears as though escaping the depths of hell. In suffering, he opens the tomb, not in glory, but on the contrary, he expresses torment. I ask for clarity, or I may be missing something. Jesus unravels the meaning:

Pains of Life

In truth, you are not meant to escape this world's pains but to transform them. That was my work and the cause for opening the tomb, and that is what the vision is showing.

The opening of the tomb was not my doing. It was not my work. Through living and dying, my work expresses in the charred face that you see. Taking this further, my suffering and death, indeed, were horrific to behold. However, steadfast, in my service to the Father, was the way to my rising. And so that is why the depiction I give you is haunting. The message here is that 'not all is as it seems.'

On the earthly realm, you see the glory of the Risen Christ, and you rejoice. However, you do not understand when things come your way, and they do not appear to be so good. You say, 'I am not here to suffer and experience pain,' but that is not necessarily the case. You have not known how to change the world due to the loss of my word and wisdom.

The martyrs themselves had tremendous gifts of the Spirit. They knew that if they suffered, it was for a higher purpose. They knew it not merely in their minds; they knew it in their hearts. All that I handed down made complete sense to them, and they accessed their inner power. Those holding high seats could not understand, and because of their firmness, they were in fear of them. Consequently, they were more determined to stomp out anyone who dared to walk in my name.

Now, I am not saying the Father plans that you should suffer to win your way back into heaven. Instead, you are not necessarily meant to escape life's pains but to transform the suffering.

When I came, I intended to open the doors to humanity's highest potentials. First, to relieve the anxieties, predominantly humanity's fear of God, and teach new means for accessing one's greatest strength. I primarily helped others to see that the Father makes them in his likeness. In them resides the wisdom of the Father. And to access that inner stability, they must align themselves with the heart of the Father. Here is the posturing of spiritual might.

Do remember that I put back the ear of Malchus. I never taught my followers to use their muscles to maim. Yet, those in fear of them used their minuscule power to crush my loved ones. All for their selfish greed and glory and what they would consider their precious thrones. Throughout history, you see how their glorious thrones were seized and trotted over.

Lust for power and control has led the way into one battle after another, and still to another conqueror and more destruction. Yet, the golden message I left behind is of the mightiest force beyond conquering; that is and will forever be the force of love. To love as the Creator loves closes the distance between the Father and his people.

I do not place heavy burdens or expectations on my followers. Rather, my work is opening the way and allowing the light of the Father to speak for itself. I lead my followers into the Father's light because I experience in the light the oneness with the Father.

Although many understood my words as blasphemous, others realized the Father's light. For them, my truth illuminates the soul by awakening the seed of my Father's light in them. Blessed are those who hear. They are those whose hearts are open to the Spirit of the Father. Their souls awaken to the sound of my truth.

Jesus, to whom are you referring when you talk about "...their precious thrones"? Are you talking about history before or after your passing?

> Your history continues. Do you not see it in today's world on a different scale? How many times have you resounded the cliché, 'Men trampling over men, all for selfish gain!' The point is a reference to the history of human thinking and the fear that motivates it. I understand; however, humanity is challenged to meet a higher level of concern. You have reached a precipice, and the time is upon you to decide the path ahead.

I am taken back to a theology class while discussing attributes of God, and the professor raised the subject of God's life expanding. Although a stimulating conversation, it's a hidden mystery. I mention this because I have since learned that God's life grows. However, we did not conceive of the possibility that God's life expands through us. Yet is that not what heaven on earth is all about? Here, human potential explodes. Through our finite existence, God with us creates the potential to expand God's life. Hence, Jesus' message, "The kingdom of God is at hand."

To be clear, for humans to create heaven on earth is the God-given potential to expand God's life. It's interesting to note, however, God is not focusing on expansion. Instead, God focuses on the joy of loving, while the expansion is the outcome of the Father's love. We have missed seeing how profoundly precious the mysteries of God and the kingdom Jesus proclaimed!

Of course, Jesus did not put it that way. Instead, he talks about the treasures of God's giving. The "parable of the talents" is the most exciting and revealing of all. Jesus uses the story of a Master giving from the treasury of his wealth measured in the weight of gold, copper, or silver. Through it, Jesus is delivering the message that life should not be hoarded but is for sharing as God shares God's life with us. If not, we are lifeless. Therefore, the Master tells the one who, because of fear, buries what he is given, will lose even the little he has (Mt 25:24-25). The Father does not want us to be in fear, but in love. Fear has nowhere to go. On the other hand, love has everywhere to be and to build.

Today, the world is in a crisis, and, if nothing else, we are having a taste of what he is saying. I am pointing to the kingdom that we are intended to become. The greatest of all treasures are from the giving of God on which we must build. Although many know God, they do not realize the Father's giving and many in fear put the kingdom on hold. Perhaps you are beginning to understand why.

God serves all, and he does not speak in lofty words. Instead, his language is plain and simple. Yet, we bind ourselves with many laws and rules, and the Father's treasures hide behind judgments, confusion, and fears flowing from worldly professionalism in God's name.

You can see all the rules surrounding certain practices for yourself, especially when speaking of marriage or participating in a wedding in or outside the Church. Intellectual litanies define who should and should not attend, and why you should not. The ordinary person is not wrapped up in an academic realm of "do's and don'ts," nor is God. God intends that we are in love, not fear. When living in God's love, you do not need a book of laws and rules to tell you what is right and wrong. That is a distortion shaped by fear. Love is always right and knows what is not.

That is the measure God places in our hearts here with us now, but many are anesthetized because the intellectual world often hampers the spirit within. Many, if not most, get stuck in the realms of human reasoning and lose sight of God's divine heart. Remember, Jesus picked twelve fishermen to be his closest followers. He stood away from the academic world of Scribes and Pharisees who were less disposed to Jesus' divine inspiration. History conveys the extent of their rebuke.

Elders of the Synagogue educated in the prescriptions of the law were predominately fixed in their belief system. Hence, they were not open to Jesus' teachings and certainly not accepting him as one with the Father. Jesus' birth into an ordinary family within a humble setting sets the tone for revealing the void between Jesus and the authority figures of the Church. Instead, Jesus called those compatible with his heart so that others could see high seats and lofty rituals mean little to God. Contrarily, the Jewish Elders leaned on purification rites through the washing of hands, cups, and bowls.

Jesus picked his apostles carefully to demonstrate God's basis for acceptance has little to do with self-righteous rhetoric and practices flowing from exterior values. God desires the interior values that flow from love and humility that reflect the truth of our Maker's heart.

Jesus knew their potential as well as their fears. We say today, "All there is, is love." We can be sure Jesus knew this to be true in every word he spoke. Hence, the reason I say his words are often blurred in the scriptures is because men's fears taint them. I am not saying that to blame, but that was the unfortunate progression of Jesus' truth as we have it today.

We all have fears, yet countless people are not in touch with them. In recent years, much has been written about the topic. For those unaware yet interested in knowing more, you may be amazed at the extent of the issue. When questioning others, I cannot tell the numbers who respond in a huff, "I'm not afraid of anything." Ironically, the huffing alone springs from fear.

I am sure the fathers of the Church were misled by their fears. To think God needed their defense turned out to be a grave offense against humanity and God. Jesus told Peter to put down his sword. He saw his followers as vessels of the Father's light, while the early Church fathers saw themselves as "defenders of the faith." The impetus was fear and control. Yet, above all, Jesus came to alleviate humanity's fears, not redirect them.

Jesus' mission was far more significant than dying for our sins. Indeed, fear is a severe adversary, and Jesus shows the way by teaching us to put down our swords and direct ourselves into the light. Now, the tall order is on us!

As you can see, this is no fluffy walk. As Jesus says, his truth is not printed on a page but etched in the hearts of his followers. The more we bond on the ground of God's love, the less fear has its way. Right now, fear is doing a number on us. Jesus has shown us the way, and that is the only way!

The conflict between fear and love is longstanding. In the "parable of the talents," Jesus portrays the dynamic. In opposition to fear, our love has the potential to grow in the Father's life. That is the holy essence of the kingdom Jesus proclaims.

I recall an exceptional portrayal of the Holy Spirit, as presented while studying at St. John's Seminary College, Boston, MA. Eloquently framed: The Holy Spirit is the bubbling over of love between the Father and the Son. I recall it here because it expresses the idea of God's life expanding through love. Furthermore, the idea surfaced again when studying at St. Mary's Seminary & University, Baltimore, MD. The margin between the references offers a significant witness to divine truth.

To put this in another way, the "bubbling over" of divine love is God with us, and so to the kingdom at hand. And with that, signifying the potential to grow in God's life. Far less than a judge, the Father persistently calls us to the task of love, which is the way now and always. To love has many forms and many ways challenging. We must remember, love is the fire of the universe. Nothing prevails against it, yet many challenges, as you see in the divides playing out in the world.

Although we cannot fully comprehend the meaning beneath the paradigm I speak of, that is expected. The Father's action is love, and from God's love comes the expansion of life. The idea cannot be analyzed within the mind's limits but only understood within one's heart and soul. Here is why the kingdom is a mystery held from the seeing of many. In the Gospel of John, Jesus talks about knowing the Father through him because the Father lives within him, and later hints about the paradigm he sets into motion.

> Very truly, I tell you, the one who believes in me will also do the works that I do and, in fact, will do greater works than these, because I am going to the Father (Jn 14:12).

Father, I ask, might there be something to say that would help us see beneath the meaning of Jesus' words?

> I see the truth of my Son in each person, but they do not see it in themselves, and that is why he was sent that they would see. Again, many are blind and cannot see. If they could, they would see the truth in these words and find their way into a new order.

Clearly, you are speaking about our path into the kingdom. Am I right to say that the greater things we will do point to the kingdom Jesus spoke of?

Indeed, the entire human endeavor is to build on earth
as it is in heaven. Was this not written in Jesus' prayer?

Of course, it misleads because the problem of sin and evil
circumvents the prayer. To pray as such is not wrong. However, it
builds on fears we have not resolved instead of the light Jesus
reveals. Or might I say, we have not understood God's saving love?

No sense to look back at this point. The time is for
moving forward. The prayers have supported the care of
the Father, but not to the extent of how close I am to
each one.

Your words remind me of Jesus' metaphor of a hen caring for
her young when conveying the extent of your care for each one. I
see in his words the depth of truth. Truly, your Spirit is with us, yet
I feel the enemy is at our door.

You have but one enemy, and yes, fear surrounds you,
all of you; do not be afraid to be who you are. See in
yourselves the power of my Spirit and know you are
safe. Do not hide, instead stand up and build what you
are here to build.

However, a note of caution, the enemy is cunning and hides
behind the rhetoric of authorities and false promises. The posture is
not just about church authorities, but leadership across all spectrums
of life. In retrospect, no haven is safer than the realm of God's
kingdom. Jesus pointed to the kingdom of the Father's love where
fear may threaten but never subdue or put asunder. In another way,

the goodwill of creation will never lose to the ill will of men or women, and all that is not of God's intention will lose even the little that is given.

At this juncture, I question how many realize God's safekeeping through instruments of penances and various acts of repentance. Of course, God's love is acknowledged. However, the practices generally press against the idea of sin and the foil of human weakness. On the other hand, the emphasis shifts when talking about God's light with us. The Father expresses his view in this way:

> Because practices involving sin and repentance intend to connect people to my love and forgiveness, the act is not without merit. However, I offer more to my children than the static language of forgiveness. I seek to encourage my children with the strength of my love. Not to take over the world but to sweep the globe with loving intent and transformation. However, you miss the point if you are busy only preparing yourselves for heaven.
>
> Opposed to creating heaven on earth, you are on a merry-go-round that does not build what you are here to establish. The kingdom is in your hands. I give you the strength to create. Already, you have all that you need. But you do not act because you believe within the depths of your heart that you are not worthy to enter heaven, let alone be yourselves heaven's makers.

The Father illustrates the power of his loving intent for sweeping transformation across all boundaries. Here, I pause because it speaks to the core of my experience when witnessing what is not happening in many churches – the very reason I went into seclusion. Practices in penance may offer forgiveness, but that does not mean God's acceptance. In effect, many walk away feeling like sinners, especially when believing that nothing in them has changed. If those of a similar mind have nothing more to take from this work, may they loudly hear the voice of the Father's loving and transformative intent!

And what is more transformative than God's unconditional embrace? For many, to proclaim God's loving intent and transformation is overdue. Here, the Father beautifully and skillfully places before me his solemn truth, and my heart is at peace.

I am taken once again to the moment of saying "yes" to my calling. I recall how I wished to shake the world with the love that has rocked my world! Here is the unfolding of Jesus' truth when speaking about the kingdom of God. "The kingdom of heaven is like a treasure hidden in a field, which someone found and hid; then in his joy he goes and sells all that he has and buys that field" (Mt 13:44).

Like the man Jesus speaks of, I left all that I had with a burning desire to share the treasure of God's truth. In the Gospel of John, Jesus commissioned his apostles to show love to one another as he had shown to them (Jn 13:34). They did not go forward with laws and rules or attempt to draft a blueprint on how they should proceed, but to tell their story of God's love. As the kingdom overflows in me, the joy is overwhelming, and I wish only to carry the treasure into the world. Although clutter from past notions confuses the way, the Father and the Son intend to clear the path.

Respecting Creation

Animation of the Frog

The scene of an enchanting frog sitting on a beautifully shaped lily pad opens like a curtain. Rich in color, the natural forest greens paint a view oozing with aromas and the freshness of life. Looking straight at me with big glistening eyes, I see the expression of its friendly grin. The Father narrates:

> All creatures of the earth and skies, seas and rivers, lakes and shores, lands and mountains, and every terrain are from my hands. What you would perceive as good, bad, and ugly, but all serving a higher purpose. The marvel is a journey wrapped in mystery and all fashioned in love. You see, all life is by my design, and I love all things; such is why you must respect all life.
>
> Humanity has not a sense of such respect for all life. I do not understand. This cannot be any longer; because if humanity does not respect all things, they are self-destructing. What will be, will be in respect of all things. A new world builds on respect for all things beginning with one another.
>
> As believed by many, to see me in all things is no crime. Did my Son ever say or see it that way? He did not classify the created order. On the contrary, he saw

God's wisdom in all creation. When telling the story of the sparrow's fall, Jesus is speaking of my intimate connection with all nature that even a sparrow will not fall without my knowing. He sees no crime in viewing God connected to all creatures and all creation.

Father, you speak eloquently about all things of your making and that you are a part of all things.

I am, of course, but I do not expect many to understand. The misunderstanding has passed through centuries, and few have sought to see a higher perspective.

As I review the history, especially Paul's poor perception of himself and then pressing on humanity, his theological outlook errs on the dark side. In retrospect, we can hardly see the truth of God's nature, and might I say oneness with all creation. I would think all life, all creation is sacred. If that is correct, we are the ones who desecrate it unnecessarily due to ignorance and choices that flow from the dark side of our nature.

I turn to St. Francis, who saw you in all creation. He perceived sister moon and brother sun and spoke to the animals and even the fish. Did he not know of your oneness with all things? Why is his legacy missing from our theological outlook? I raise many questions with many things on my mind and heart.

Fear not to question, no matter how many there are, for I am not human with a limited mind or bearing. First, let me say that yes, humans have a dark side as I have a dark side. However, there exists a difference, most do not know. Many are learning to balance the dark and the light, while I Am in perfect balance. Some may ask, 'Why is this?' Although not meant for the human mind to comprehend, both energies fuel creation.

Might I say one cannot exist without the other?

You could, but the equation is more complicated than that, for what you perceive is the outcome, not the cause and effect. About your questions concerning the difference between human nature and my presence in all things, try appreciating this parable:

The human walks on two feet by design and purpose. Monkeys also have two feet. However, with arms so large and strapping, they swing from limb to limb across the jungle. Perfect creatures in function and design, they are fantastic. The elephants are incredibly fascinating and altogether different. Massive in size and ability, they rumble through the jungle and shake the earth.

I could go on about the mystery you see in all things and the love that propels the animals, but I share these thoughts to lay out a brief picture beneath the surface. Their creation is not about what every animal is to accomplish. Instead, their purpose is to serve the vision that flows from my heart. Yes, you see it as a food chain, hence an image of the dark and the light and how they co-exist. Acutely aware, the animals live in that projection, and they do so boldly and beautifully. Like humans, they have many instincts and feelings, but their responsibility for creation is nil. However, they exist to satisfy me and stimulate humankind's perceptions.

Although many appear as savages, they are less blameworthy than many humans. If you learn the difference between human responsibilities and see the animal kingdom placed in your care and justifiable use, your world may be the paradise that you seek. So yes, I am a part of all things, but all things, as you know, can never be as I Am.

To be sure, you are saying the animals serve a purpose and intend to exist just as they are?

Do you see the difference?

We can be who we wish to be for better or worse, given our free choice. Although humanity perceives differences between animals and humans, the distinction is based solely on human reasoning and less divine purpose. The idea has not fully taken hold in our technological age and does not reflect the majority's mentality. Indeed, you demonstrate that the animal world also serves a divine purpose in its profound service to creation, especially in supporting humanity's physical and spiritual well-being. By God's love and design, we must exercise gratitude and care for creation and all creatures in this regard.

Moreover, through the royal gift of free will, our purpose is to bring forth your life force to enhance the created order. Therefore, to engender harmony by exercising our love for all things. Here, I display the art of the kingdom and the expansion of your life for creating new earth.

All creatures are my creation and fuel the grandeur of life in their service to life. Their beauty and eloquence are services for building character. They are poetry that soothes the soul. Do you hear the songs of the birds or even the crickets? All are in service to illuminate the imagination of humans. Therefore, stimulating the soul to reach beyond the mind's limits and into the mystery I Am.

Humanity cannot perceive animals as unimportant to the abounding enterprise of creation. Although appearing as a lesser consideration, recall the abuses to my creatures, lands, skies, and seas. You know a book could be written and many are already on the shelves.

St. Francis knew of your connection to all things and was able to speak to the animals, birds, and fish. His engagement is unprecedented. What lesson ought we learn from him?

Many lessons, but to learn only this one is enough. All life, all things are sacred because I Am their Maker.

Undoubtedly, one could write another book about our lack of understanding.

Jesus Psalm

Lyric of the Father's Light

What is the light, if not the light of the Father's love?
What is more genuine and trustworthy than the light that flows from the Father's heart?

He is the sun that shines
The rains that fall from the skies
He is the wellspring that pours into the oceans
Through him, your waters are rich
Through him, the soils filter and breed life
Through him, all things are made, and
Fashioned from the purity that flows from his heart

Jesus, is this meant metaphorically or as a mystery?

Both a mystery and metaphorically, for you cannot know the full expression of God, but All that is!

Jesus continues

Why this has not been understood through the centuries is mind-boggling. For us to look down on the earth and see, we cry tears that you have not been able to understand. How precious and pure God's love is, transforming all things. His is the light to all that is. Most importantly, his light intends to shine on you, beloved humans. You are his most valuable possession, and he does not possess you as a toy.

My message did not reach you. The Father possesses you in the recesses of his heart where there is only love for you. We desire that the ground of the Father's love resurfaces, as I, Jesus, raised his passion to the surface.

Through the Father's favor, I came to you and the Father through me. The Son's love is for the Father and you, brothers and sisters. That is who you are, and in each one, I see the Father's light. But people do not see what I see, and they cannot understand. They are in darkness, so I came in light so that people's eyes would open. And as you can see, the light dims, and the kingdom does not come.

My prayer was, 'Thy will be done on earth as it is in heaven.' The Father intends that his life shines through creation, but it only can be through you! Hence, do you see the power of free will? A precious gift that cannot be measured humanly but comes with the cost of choosing wisely. By opening the way into the Father's heart, I stoked my followers' desire to love respectfully.

The Mountain Jesus Moved

Skyscraper

I stand on the sidewalk, looking straight up as far as I can see above the massive skyscraper. Nestled amid a beautiful and bustling city, the unimaginable panorama surrounding me holds my attention to the majestic views shimmering under the umbrella of a clear blue sky. Fading into the distant horizon, I feel as small as a dot, yet as entranced as a child in a toy shop. Jesus narrates:

Opening the Gates

> Progress has led humankind to new elevations through its productive use of resources, including advanced human ingenuity. However, earthen treasures (resources) that fuel the industry are lost to its greed in the process. The same happens with my 'word' passing through history and my cause losing to human reasoning.
>
> Often the resurgence of a plan becomes more prevalent and richer in meaning and fiery in momentum. And that is what must happen now. Indeed, I am here with you, all of you, and not in just one place. I am for the life of the world, and so my Spirit, my energy, my rising, reaches new heights as I rise in those who

embrace me. I raise myself in those who receive me in love and act in love. I come to those who hear my word and understand why I come.

I am not to judge but to open the way to the Father's life. I wish to make it clear that I came to breathe life into this world, and I did so by proclaiming, 'The kingdom of God is at hand.' Like a skyscraper reaching up into the sky, my proclamation was the tolling of the bell reaching new heights in the hearts of my followers. Over time, those heights have been strained and lost. I am not talking about the spread of Christianity across the globe. I am talking about where the spread of Christianity was to take humanity.

Many believe in me because of the spread; however, they believe in me and less in themselves. That is not where I intended to take humanity.

My intention for all people is the same as mine for the disciples. It was always to help humanity see that they are indeed sons and daughters of one Father. His light is with you. So, you see how my message loses to the dark corners of misinformation. Subsequently, as you focus on unremitting efforts to overcome sin, you are falsely led into paths breeding guilt and shame. As a result, the attempts weigh on the soul's fear of God.

The gates I open are the gates of your hearts that you would see and build on brotherhood and sisterhood. Was that not the intention of the two greatest commandments? The foundation may have been buried in time, but its truth still stands. On this foundation, you must build. Upon it, you experience the strength of my Spirit and the joy within your souls. As you realize the kingdom that is within, you will know the way by seeing through your hearts.

God's extraordinary giving to humanity is to magnify. Unfortunately, because of the misinterpretations of Jesus' cross, many are suppressed by the problem of sin and live with a poor sense of self and God. The mixed feelings flow for many reasons, and none are from God.

In retrospect, many feel like they have empty pockets. God is not asking us to jump through hoops. He sent his Son so that we would know his love and acceptance and respond in kind. Yet, this is less the distinguishing image of God through the Son. Jumping through hoops of any kind means little to God if not propelled by the love that moves us.

Opposed to his death on a cross, the culmination of Jesus' saving action came through the in-breaking of the Father's love, the greatest miracle of all. And it was not in a single moment but through every word and deed Jesus expressed. He said, "I am the way," not meaning his cross, but personifying the love of God in his every breath. Misinterpreting his cross provokes the pains of oppression, confusion, and anger, none for which he died except to bring love forward. What is more significant than laying down his life for a world in fear of God and those propelling the fear? And again today, the Father's plea resounds that we may hear the truth of God's heart.

Scripture reveals, "No one has greater love than this, to lay down one's life for one's friends" (Jn 15:13). However, we have not understood the ground of God's love for which Jesus laid down his life. Inseparable from the kingdom, the ground of the Father's love is the essence of the kingdom. Hence, the "kingdom with us now," while the meaning of "not yet complete," concerns our disposition.

The incompletion is on us. The truth is conveyed in the scriptures. Once Jesus was asked by the Pharisees when the kingdom of God was coming, and he answered:

> The kingdom of God is not coming with things that can be observed; nor will they say, 'Look, here it is!' or 'There it is!' For, in fact, the kingdom of God is among you (Lk 17:20-21).

The extent of this is blurred by outdated misconceptions that hinder the breadth of Jesus' message. Consequently, opposed to living in the direction of Jesus' life-giving truth, we have been trying to fix the problem of sin for over two thousand years. Jesus' passion was then, and is now, to bring forward the Father's love, intending to gather the "Lost Sheep." Instead, we are scattered, and many are still searching.

Lost to the actions and reasoning of men, our most precious treasure is buried. Unable to retrieve it, in fear, the Church fathers turned to obsessions of power and control. Consequently, the twist in perception derails Jesus' truth, and we return to the oppression of guilt, shame, and fear that he came to help us overcome. And so, Father, after two thousand years with a heart that still sorrows, you cry out, "I paid a great price in the blood of my Son, why do you still persecute me?" I did not know then the nature of your cry, but I know now. How different our world, if only we knew, the mountain of fear Jesus moved. Father, may I ask why you waited so long to get our attention?

> The question is not about why I wait so long to cry out but to wait for someone who would hear and make a difference.

How many extraordinary Saints since Jesus' passing, and beloved Pope John Paul II?

> More than good reason, it takes a loving heart and time
> for the right moment when people will listen both
> outside and inside the churches.

The Father's clarion call is to love and for those who have ears to hear. But how does anyone hear when humanity's most valuable treasure hides in the mayhem of time and misunderstanding? Is not our most precious gift the Father's love? And to realize the Father's genius is not in any way expressed in negative energies of wrath. The Father creates from the abyss; God is not unleashing more chaos. Instead, God's nature is *Love,* and we are of God's nature, called to love. In that light, we pick up our mats and walk.

Faith in Oneself

Jesus says, "Many believe in me because of the spread of Christianity; however, they believe in me and less in themselves. That is not where I intended to take humanity." Here, I refer to Peter's story when he saw Jesus's walking on water. The scene in the Gospel of Mark is exceptionally provocative. Jesus intended to walk right past his disciples. One might think Jesus was showing off or playing with them. However, we know this was not the case.

Commentators will say they cannot be sure exactly what happened on the water that day. The Gospel of Mark 6:48 reads, "He intended to pass them by." Some commentators suggest that Jesus was testing his disciple's faith. Therefore, typically, we have another event to display his followers' lack of faith. But even here, if that is true, it also presents Jesus' relentless will to teach them far more than to test them. As such, this gets to the core of what happened that day.

When reflecting on this remarkable event, it may appear to some that Jesus had tricked his disciples (Mt 14:29). Why did he call Peter out to the water? What was the lesson Jesus was teaching? Was it about faith? Well, what kind of faith? Was it the kind that maintains focus on Jesus? I say with certainty that Jesus knew Peter would sink! However, Jesus was not about poking fun or hurting him. Rather, Jesus knew that Peter possessed the potential and could and would walk on water.

I spent much of my life looking at this passage from a realistic vantage point. Often, I pondered that no records exist of anyone, not even the greatest saints, walking on water. Even St. Francis of Assisi, whose life is so carefully recorded, although he talked to the animals, birds, and fish, and may have walked on rooftops; he never walked on water.

Well then, if that is the case and this event is not a game, what was Jesus teaching Peter? Perhaps, he was presenting to his disciples the profound truth that we are capable of the extraordinary in faith. In faith, we can rise above all things and truly walk over the fears, troubles, and worries that can quickly engulf us.

Realistically, our attention span comes with its limitations. For anyone to remain focused is enormously difficult! Hence, from another perspective, Peter's failure to walk on the sea is understandable, that "no" he was not focusing on Jesus. Instead, it's more revealing that the Christ he did not see was not Jesus who stood before him but the Spirit of Christ that lived within him. Hence, he was distracted by doubts and fears, which became his focus. Jesus was teaching him to take hold of the Spirit of God within. He demonstrates to Peter and the others how real the potential to embrace their sonship with the Father "is".

More than keeping their focus on Jesus, something much bigger was at work here. What exactly does it mean when we say, "We must keep our focus on Jesus?" How humanly possible is it anyway? We would all sink in the waves and winds of life that assail us. If they are to successfully sail the ship of Jesus' truth into the world, the apostles had to prevail against much stormier seas. Most would agree that the sea Peter failed to walk upon was nothing compared to the storm of his cross and the trials that he would later face.

In all that we do in life, our most significant obstacles are not the things that stand outside of us but the things we hold within us. We are the ones who stand in our way! Doubt and fear are the foremost threats to hinder human potential. Sometimes they are easy to identify; however, they often flow from seeds deeply planted.

When Peter failed to walk on water, he failed to believe in himself. He failed to stand on the inner strength of the Father's life with him! Jesus believed in him! Jesus saw in him the life of the Father. Jesus told him to come! Peter did not fail to put his faith in Jesus at all. He stepped out of the boat! If anything, all his confidence was in Jesus. However, he was the one who had to walk over the water. When realizing this, he was swallowed up by his fears and doubts. If his faith was not in Jesus, why would he have left the boat at the start? If his faith was not in Jesus, why did he reach out to him when sinking?

I said earlier; we are led to believe that we have faith and understanding down to a science when in truth, we do not. And for some, it will be a struggle just as it was for the apostles.

The storm presents us with an important message not to miss. Jesus was teaching his disciples not to be entirely dependent on him. Of course, they needed him, and so too do we need him. However,

Jesus needed them to carry his truth over the waters that would assail them. Mandatory for that task, they first needed to bathe in the waters of the Father's trust. They had to experience how intimately they were tied to the Father, and the Father to them.

The Father would have it no other way. He loved them. The Father's desire was for their success, and so too for ours. Jesus says, "…the Father's will be done on earth as it is in heaven." The Father intends that we come to realize the fullness of our connection as daughters and sons for the greater good of creation.

Coming to believe is one thing; learning to exercise one's belief in oneself is another. The apostles had to learn to walk on their own. As much as Jesus loved them and taught them, he could not carry their crosses for them, any more than he can carry ours. They had to believe in themselves, but that could only be when trusting how deeply the Father loved them.

Indeed, they would carry their crosses to death, and the strength had to come from within them. It was this inner strength that attracted thousands more to follow. The fact that Jesus cannot carry our crosses has not changed. Jesus teaches us to have faith in his way and his word, but this falls short of the mark if faith in ourselves does not follow. How many gifted people, smart people, and incredible people fail because they sink into self-doubt and fear? I see it almost every day!

PART 5

Resurrecting Jesus' Truth

Divine Awakening

Unconditional Love

Thundering Waterfall

As though lifting a curtain, Jesus begins, "I present the showing of a waterfall's immense size and power." Immediately, it came to me: Crashing straight down from the colossal height of a mountainside, it displays both the might to destroy and the power to refresh and give life. Jesus narrates:

Listening to *Your Soul*

> My Father's breath is like the strength of a waterfall. Some may place their lives on a thin line, like those who walk on tight ropes to cross to the other side. Some elect to harness the energy for producing electricity or channel the flow for irrigation or domestic supply. And then, some dare to take on the challenge of jumping into the falls. But, as you know, they are few and so are the casualties.
>
> Yet, none of that diminishes its might. Instead, those who approach walk with caution. Nay! They exercise a lot of caution! They do not recklessly lunge themselves into the waterfall. When coming into such force, one typically approaches with prudence.

Many walk unconsciously. Not realizing the force of my Father's hand, they taunt; you might say when they dare to take chances that risk their souls' life. Yet, they do not know they walk a thin line. Instead, they step forward with little to no discretion. For them, they learn the hard way, and the journey is long and painful. Nevertheless, that will not stop the Father from offering opportunities for growth and change. A door opens to them, and still, the choice is theirs.

To risk the life of one's soul is to take the gift of life for granted. Life is a miraculous gift meant to be spent in many profound and powerful ways, each one according to his or her talents. God gives all for the coloring of life, therefore, to put into practice your gifts in alignment with your soul's purpose. To deny your soul stands in the way of the Father's giving and the world around you.

On the other hand, many put forward efforts to be as they understand God wishes them to be, but they are led astray by those who do not know the bounty of the Father's love. I speak not just about the power of God's love, but the immensity of God's breath. Here, underlying the extraordinary depth of the Father's unconditional love.

Are you saying that the depth of God's unconditional love is often denied, therefore, creating pitfalls for those choosing to follow their hearts?

Indeed, I am. In effect, do you see the consequences of unspoken burdens placed on the hearts of my people and the restraint for freely walking in one's truth?

Of course, but I have not heard from that perspective.

Many lead God's people with perceptions that do not align God's people with Jesus' truth. For them, the Father weeps. In this vision, Jesus opens wide the doorway into the Father's heart, and etches the message on my soul that such suffering does not have to be anymore. Here, God expresses his desire to release his people from all that weighs on them and enlightens those who keep the gate from opening.

The entrance to the Father's heart is revealed by the Son. For many, the passage is blocked with bars that invalidate the soul's life. And so, it was that over thirty years ago, the Father etched the words into my heart, "I paid a great price in the blood of my Son, why do you still persecute me?"

Consciously or not, some leaders, in God's name do not acknowledge the depths of God's love and acceptance. Instead, they amplify human weakness and betray God's kingdom. The problem runs deep on levels of high and low. Yet, no matter how small, the soul feels the wound. And, the question lingers, how long will it take to mend? While denying God's intentions, willfully or not, people are hurting, and so too God and God's kingdom.

The Father wills for the kingdom set upon the foundation of his love. The idea is not obscure, and people know its truth. What is the basis for the cliché "What would Jesus do?" If anything except to see through the eyes of God's love, that is not what Jesus would do. You can find that place in your heart; ever so simple. If you walk in the direction of the Father's light, what more do you need to decide for the greater good?

And if you should stray, pick yourself up and redirect yourself into the Father's light. I profess no room for guilt, shame, or fear in God's direction. Remember, you are a work in progress. Do you feel yourself moving forward or not? Growth is not about having any challenges or perceived setbacks but a better posture to see and resolve.

Speaking of challenges and posturing, I wrote about what makes God awesome long ago. God can give and take life in a single breath, or the Creator can stop the globe from spinning and the planets surrounding it. However, what makes God mighty is God's unfathomable love. The greatest gift of all, yet countless people are unable to access it. I know because I have counseled unthinkable numbers of good and faithful people. Hence, the sorrow that comes when viewing God's nature through our ancestors' lens. Who would believe that God truly and dearly loves unconditionally?

For some, to say so may sound absurd. However, if God's unconditional love cannot make a difference in someone's life, tell me then who or what can? God is the sum of anyone's meaning, and God is love. Be sure the kingdom depends on the significance of people's lives. I look out the window and see where we are landing, and sin is not the problem but the lack of love.

Yet, what more reason for anyone to bow before God and praise all life and all creation? Is God's passion not at the center of Jesus' life and death, and so too the martyrs that followed?

I once gave a talk to my congregation about the vessel we are of God's life. From the altar, I announced: The peace of God is with you! And, beneath their breath, some ask, "Well, the one next to me is a sinner, I am not. Why then is the peace of God with him or her? What difference should it make then to be with or without fault?"

I said to them that even a prison cell can sustain life. What kind of home do you seek to make of yourself for God? Is it about what others are doing or not doing or what God calls you to do? Here the question is not about sins or faults, but how crucial love is for the life of one's soul. That is everything that matters to God.

God has so much to give, not just in the temporal world but far beyond. But many are taught to get into the gates of heaven by way of purchasing a ticket. So, they go through all the motions while perceiving the heavenly reward is like another duty to perform. You are led astray to think so. The kingdom is a far more precious relationship with a loving Father. Jesus called God, "Daddy"!

This is not about heaven or hell, but how you choose to rise in God's life. You who say you love life and strive to see and experience all that you possibly can, why would you want to miss all that you can be in the Father's life? Jesus talks about many rooms in the Father's house (Jn 14:2-3). The home you make of yourself will determine the home the Father prepares for you. Who would not strive to create a beautiful home of oneself? Jesus spoke similar words, and perhaps, at times used the same exact language.

Do you see the magnitude of Jesus' message and how important the treasure you carry is? No force in the entire universe is more powerful than God's love. And unconditionally, God loves us. Love is the power God places in our hands that we may carry in our hearts. To embrace the Father's love is the fuel for transformation and the genuine wings of the soul. Transformative love is a snapshot image of God and the extraordinary image that shapes us. However, opposed to actualizing God's unconditional and transformative love, we are limited by fears. As a result, one might take note of where we are heading.

The message of the "Waterfall" reveals the martyrs' foundation of strength, as illustrated on the walls of the catacombs. Telling the story Jesus etches in their hearts, the martyrs' hymn is forever inscribed within the walls of their ancient hiding place. The "Hymn of the Catacombs" reflects the souls of the martyrs: [10]

O GLADSOME LIGHT

O gladsome Light,
O Grace of God the Father's face,
th' eternal splendor wearing;
celestial, holy, blest,
our Savior Jesus Christ,
joyful in Thine appearing!

Now, as day fadeth quite,
we see the evening light,
our wonted hymn outpouring;
Father of might unknown,
Thee, His incarnate Son,
and Holy Ghost adoring.

To Thee of right belong
all praise of holy songs,
O Son of God, Life-giver;
Thee, therefore, O Most High,
the world does glorify
and shall exalt forever. [11]

---

[10] Liderbach, Daniel *Christ in the Early Christian Hymns,* Paulist Press, Mahwah, NJ, 1998, (Chapter IV, pages 50-51).

[11] Author Anonymous, Source: Greek Phos Hilaron c. 200, Translated by Robert Seymour Bridges 1899, Hymns to the Living God #343.

https://hymnary.org/hymn/HTLG2017/343

Jesus is named "Gladsome Light" because the martyrs understood him as the splendor of the Father with them, less the "Lamb that is slain" for sin, but the "Giver of Life." The martyrs were not riding on forgiveness but on God's goodness and love for his children exemplified in the Son. The life he gives is the Father's light. Here reflects the Son's true image, who passes on the flame of the Father's light. In this work, the light passes on to you who have ears to hear and an open heart to receive the light of Christ.

Today, many Christians suffer at a distance from God, and fewer have an open heart to the Father. Although the Hymn shines a light on the Father's heart, conversely, it also reveals the depths of the Father's anguish because of the fear and control that holds many away. Hence, the Father cries, "I paid a great price in the blood of my Son. Why do you still persecute me?"

God is Not Distant

Jesus and the Dish

I took a moment to sit back at my desk when caught unsuspectingly. Plain and simple, the image of a dish came to me, yes, a "dish." In a lyric, Jesus continues:

Solid Ground

The dish is breakable, and likewise the human is fragile. Often you think not, but delicate you are, and many hide behind a hard shell. Although uncomfortable, you hide anyway because exposing yourself is often more painful.

So, one must ask why? Of what are you afraid? And, the truth is, you are afraid of one another. You're afraid of an insult, a negative comment, or criticism, and why is that?

For one reason, you do not know yourself. You may know that you are shy. You may even know that you are hiding behind something. However, that does not mean because you know such things that you are fully aware of yourself. So, how does one know oneself?

The matter is one of self-acceptance and knowing something much more profound exists within acceptance. And this is where I ushered in the greatest miracles of all. I helped my followers to understand and not just to say who they are but also to bring it out of them. And so, what am I suggesting?

I can say I helped them know they are sons and daughters of God, and that the Father's Spirit is with them. To be in the company of God is not a myth, and hardly something in the distance. God is a genuine presence to experience. And in the experience, the company of God illuminates the truth of who you are.

In the image of the dish, you have a tool for transcending your weaknesses. See them, acknowledge them, and place them in the Father's hands. Experience how your weaknesses can be your greatest strengths.

When handing over our weaknesses, you are not advocating what many perceive as a crutch. How are we to understand this?

The Father Intervenes

For many, their fears stand in the way of my love for them. I do not mean to be a crutch. Humans must learn the responsibility to love. Love has many forms and, like a seedling, needs to grow. Rules and misunderstanding often sit on the seeds of love planted within the soul, and they do not bear fruit. The seeds I sow are of my heart that indeed bear fruit. Knowing you are loved is the ground of your strength, not for harm but to freely create from your heart the world for which you wish.

Many withhold secrets deep inside. This act is not healthy for the life of the soul. I affirm that fears are the reasons why. We do not trust each other because of our fears, and many have learned to hide them from God. Some souls are stuck, and some remain stuck to the end of their lives. Such anguish is unnecessary when thinking of hiding anything from the Father.

The issue is not the Father, but in such cases, many do not know God, which creates a significant problem affecting not just individuals but whole communities. Again, Jesus sets our souls free from oppression. As it was, I regret to speak of the extent of suffering that permeated the Christian communities following Jesus' death. And still, the foundation is not on solid ground. The Father wants his children to know him and to live freely in him. To be free in the Father's truth is the theme within Jesus' messages and has been lost in the rubble of centuries.

Much division exists among people today concerning abortion. I know the act runs against the grain of respect for life. However, there are two sides to the story, and the issues are complicated and incite judgment. When an embryo is aborted, often the would-be mothers are abandoned by their communities or churches.

Seeing it from perspectives based on human reasoning is sensible to the degree that one is attempting to see from our understanding of God and creation, but often missing the mark. Consequently, some believe that God would unjustly send an unborn child to hell. Contrarily, why would the Father allow such a travesty from the beginning? The soul is God's making. Why would anyone think the Creator would give God's Spirit to a baby knowing that a part of God is going to hell? Or, at the very least, why would the Creator give of God's Spirit knowing the unborn will not be brought to full term?

God is a vital part of our lives. How many are unaware they are sacred vessels of God's presence from birth to the end? I am not saying abortions are to be congratulated, but they should not lead to judgment and condemnation. Instead, abortions should be dealt with on the level of compassion and understanding that Jesus has delivered to the world. Enough guilt and shame permeate society.

Because the choice to abort weighs heavily on the question of human values, we must ask ourselves, what are we doing to grow in our understanding? Jesus did not see judgment as a solution under any circumstances. What might we do to achieve greater good, or what might we be missing beneath the surface?

We have created enough fear in the world, and the fallout is catching up to us. The consequences are far more destructive than the many abortions. And I am not just talking about the fear that drives the choice.

During these unprecedented times, we know how difficult our world is becoming and reaching the edge. God is asking us to rethink where we came from and why we are here. The kingdom is not found in our judgments but in understanding and compassion as God is understanding and compassionate. Indeed, God intended for his kingdom to become a reflection of God's love "on earth as it is in heaven," reflecting through us. We are the temples of the Father's Holy Spirit.

Jesus had enormous faith in the human spirit. In the Gospel of John, he says, "You will do greater things than I." Unfortunately, his voice is more often trampled by the rhetoric of humans. Interestingly, on the other hand, songs are written, "What the world needs now is love, sweet love," and hearts melt, but so much is standing in our way. There is no one else to wait for but you. The earth is our home, and God makes a home of us. We have all we need.

The Father's compassion is beyond comprehension. God's unimaginable love was a stumbling block for the apostles, while Paul misinterpreted it. And Aquinas, who confronted the divine love at the end. As I wrote, Thomas' outstanding testimony is not about his philosophical and theological dissertations but the sacred vision that stopped him. Remember, when the Church came out of hiding, they embodied a posture of defense riddled in fear, far less than the Spirit of Christ. I am not judging this, but the truth should be known for the greater good. Forgiving the past is virtuous, but not changing denies the human family, no less the Father and the Son.

If I have spoken beyond my reach, I ask you, Father, please correct me.

The Father's Voice

> To speak my truth is not beyond your reach because it comes not from your head but your heart. If it should offend, that is not your doing any more than mine. My plea is a call for understanding and mercy. If anyone is denied, I Am, my beloved messenger.

Does anyone want an abortion? The impetus is fear. Have we forgotten the slaughter that continued for fifteen hundred years due to the fears of men? Where and when will our judgments end? Pope John Paul II recognized the atrocity and turned to God's forgiveness. In the summer of 1993, he publicly apologized on behalf of the Church. And his list did not end there.

The most heinous treatment of those defined as heretics were crimes against the Italian Waldensian Communities beginning as early as the fourteenth century and continuing into the early part of the nineteenth century. [12]

In 2015, Pope Francis visited the Waldensian Temple in Turin to ask forgiveness on behalf of the Catholic Church. Indeed, as I once heard, it will take us more than fifteen hundred years to get out of the mess we have created. However, as per the messages flowing from the Father's heart, it does not have to take long to be who one is called to become. God's people are ready, and they are tired and thirsty for the fullness of God's love.

Today's world illustrates how destructive our fears are, and we all have them. Is it not to wonder if the most damning force in the universe is fear? While on the other hand, the most life-giving power in the universe is love. What did Jesus teach us to exercise? In the visions, Jesus teaches that we are here to transform our fears, not create them. That is the work of the kingdom, he proclaims. Love is transformative and the most potent spiritual medicine that heals.

For years, when questioning how to love our enemies, I have never felt resolve until recently. When I asked Jesus, he replied, "When seeing your enemy's fears. You will know how to forgive."

---

[12] Wylie, J.A. , *The History of the Waldenses*, Cassell and Company 1860, copyright 2016.

Fearless Trust

Sword Standing Over the Sea

Magnificent to behold, I see the compelling vision of a sword standing straight up and towering over the deep blue sea. The blade boasts a shimmering golden cross hilt, and like a mirror, reflecting the piercing rays of golden light into the horizon and over the wavering sea. Impaled into the ocean surface, it neither sinks nor drifts left or right. Astonishingly, the signpost tells of the Father's omnipotence. Jesus continues:

Sword of Truth

> As one may read in the scriptures, I walked upon the water. As anyone knows, I should have sunk into the water. I did not. Although hard to envision, I walked upon it. I walk on water because I walk without fear. And I walk without fear because I trust in the love of the Father. Trust in the Father is my preamble to all who would follow me. To be in the Father's embrace is to be without fear and stand in strength. I am the Sword of truth.
>
> For one to rise in God's Spirit, one transcends the troubles of this world. You do not have to live in worry. I challenge you to listen to the words I speak. The Father

desires not to weigh anyone down but that you rise in his love.

Jesus always speaks in accord with the Father. Much of humankind has spent centuries repenting for their sins. The message coming through the visions tells another story. The question of repentance is not what God seeks to fulfill. God's thirst is much bigger than that. God is calling out to our hearts. When predisposed, the call is not complicated but to engage God as you are and allow God's love in return. Jesus says, "My yoke is easy," because the Father is *Love*, and he loves all creation.

Jesus came not to blame, and that is by the will of the Father. To condemn is a force driven by fear. That is not how God shapes God's children, but from love and for love. In that is the prayer for celebration and thanksgiving. Hence, revealing Jesus' charge, "… to pick up your mat and walk!"

Although the notion of God's punishment still shadows over the hearts of many, God does not punish us for our sins. God's love is greater than the best parents. What some interpret as punishment is not God's way to motivate. Sometimes, it may be God's way only to transform the direction of one's heart. In other words, all that God does, he does in love.

On the other hand, because many are misled, what they do to themselves, and others is far worse. The Father is gentle with his children. People say, "… that God gives no more than you can handle." The truth is, God gives far less than what you can manage so that you may not fall into depression and fear. Such outcomes are not God's doing; rather, they are humanity's undoing.

Here, one may also observe how truth gets lost given the work of overactive minds. On the other hand, God desires the labor of overactive hearts. Paul not only received God's mercy, but likely a seat of honor, not necessarily for his theology, but for the efforts from his heart.

Still, I am incredibly annoyed when some accentuate the notion of God's wrath and punishment when leaning into the idea that God is a "just" God, and because of that, "God will 'do' justice." When I hear those words, I often feel the ill-will beneath them, creating a double-edged sword. Indeed, God is "just," but not for revenge—instead, for transformation. The apostle Paul's life attests to that fact.

When people say, "It's all good," it indicates that we are learning to trust. However, it's not always easy because we cannot see what God sees. Nonetheless, the idea suggests that we are beginning to see that God reconciles and serves all people in multiple and multi-dimensional ways beyond explanation.

I am not claiming that trust is easy, but I have learned over time what it means to have faith. Faith can sometimes sound like a catch-all phrase or antidote, yet an authentic path that guides the way through a higher state of being. When anchored in the waters of the Father's love, one's faith stands firmly. Because we cannot see, it does not mean God's love is weak or nil; instead, it's a power within us. Jesus did not give the power of God's love to his followers but brought it out from them. He calls us to engage and express what is already with us. Hence, revealing the incompletion of the kingdom that comes through us.

Sadly, we are immersed in the ideology of law and order, right and wrong, that correlate with ideas of retribution, judgment, and punishment. Because we are a work in process and have a need for rules, the process comes with many questions and not just subduing criminal activity.

First, one might question how rightfully humanity's rules are playing out. Are they creating more turmoil than justice, more corruption than order? What do you see? Here, it raises the concern that God is left out of the process. At times, I am outraged to see innocent people prosecuted and the guilty set free; that is only a small part of the problem!

Recall the early Church in partnership with the state. If the Church was built squarely in Jesus' name, the union would have played out very differently. As it was, the Church ruled much as the state ruled. By the time the relationship was severed, there was no turning back the clock. As the bishop notes, "It took fifteen hundred years to get into this mess. It will take us much longer to get out of it." The point is that divinely inspired men and women are foundational to a genuinely just society.

I believe we would be more open to such leaders if Jesus' truth had carried through history. Right now, we are determining the road ahead, and clearly, the choice splits down the middle between love and fear. No matter how imperfect love or the extent of fear, our future is changing, and now more than ever our love matters!

Whether we reach the "Promised Land" or not is no longer a matter of waiting for God to lead us. God has already opened the way, and now it's up to us to lift the scales of fear from our eyes and see the horizon of God's life before us. God's loving intention always has been with us; however, our worries have blinded us from the beginning. That remains the story for many; however, that is not the story of the Father and the Son.

Jesus' Interjects

> Indeed, we have a different story to tell, and it unfolds
> in your hearing.

Awaken to Your Truth

Sunburst Within

Like an exploding firecracker, I see the Sunburst, its illumination igniting from the center, then spreading outward in every direction faster than the eye can capture. Unlike switching on a light, it compares more to turning up the rays of the sun. Jesus reveals:

Temples Of the Father's Light

> The image is a depiction of my power to bring light to the world. With the strength of light flashing before you, exists the magnitude of my presence bursting within your soul. The time is now to let my light that lives within you come bursting forth. My followers, the 'Sunburst' is the awakening to truth, not the truth about who I am, but the truth of who you are! You hardly know of my light bursting inside you because the darkness conceals it, and that is what I have come to lift.
>
> The darkness takes on many forms of guilt, anger, resentment, unrest, etc., and all impelled by fear. Lay down the fears they create and replace the darkness with my light. Instantly, they will fade just as the 'Sunburst' that scatters the dark. Give them to me! For this reason, I came to the world, but you have forgotten. I came to

bring light, not complexity, and gloom but to lead my Father's sheep into the light!

Again, I ask you to take the darkness that resides within you: your tears, anguish, and rejection. Name whatever haunts you, worries you, concerns you, and bring them into the light of my presence. My will is to uncloak the darkness surrounding you so that you may see the light in you. The illumination of my love and the Father's love envelops you, for you are made from light, and the light you are!

I have a job for all who hear these words. Do you know what I am asking? I am saying the world needs your light. I am not saying you must go out and preach or teach to be light for others. The action is not what they call evangelism or saving another. I am asking you only to walk in my light, and others will see; that is what I ask of you. Because you are of my Father's light and in that light, the kingdom comes, already dawning.

When Jesus speaks of "uncloaking the darkness," I turn to the hidden truth that we are a work in progress. Jesus is pointing to the idea that we are already grand beings. We are thrown off course to think that we are from the rib of Adam's side and the dust of the earth. Far more than the earth's clay, in essence, we are of the same substance of the Father. Do you see the cloak that hides you?

Many will shun the idea but do not fear; for them to actively gesture does not make them right. The soul knows what is of God and what is of humans. Stay connected to your soul, and you will know God's truth. Is it not ironic to deny, when in another breath, to say, "We are temples of the Holy Spirit?" And then to communicate with another breath that we are the earth's dust, and somehow God lives on the outside? How, then, does God make a home of us and know every hair on our heads? We are temples of God's life, not storage houses that God enters and departs.

If you genuinely believe we are temples of the Holy Spirit, why would you think differently, lest your eyes are shut, and your ears are blocked? The blessings of the visions are to unveil the darkness that your eyes may open. They intend to remove the noise of centuries that have clogged your ears, that you may hear the truth of God and the truth of you.

The Father's Voice

> To be made in my image sounds impossible to the finite human, but I am capable of the impossible. That is the miracle of your life and my life in and with you.
>
> Take not the truth of the one who writes these pages, but my truth when I say that, indeed, you are of the same substance as me. I Am the Father of all creation, and you are my children to whom I give life, and I do not give it without giving of myself.

Looking back to seminary life, I recollect a valuable precept that comes to mind. I loved the seminary, its teachings, and its teachers on both the undergraduate and graduate levels. When unpacking the theme of blindness that runs through the Gospels, my soul lifted to hear the New Testament scholar. She spoke of revelations that highlight the blindness that Jesus came to heal. Jesus was less about curing the blind eyes of men and women but opening the eyes of faith.

As with Peter's story, how many times was his faith challenged? Emphasis rests on opening the eyes of faith. However, in what or who is our faith? Are we dust or made in God's image, not as inauthentic replicas but imbued with the Spirit of God? We are here for a grand purpose, far less than making our way back to "Paradise Lost," we are called to create from the garden God has already placed within us.

Might I say again that our blindness is more about the perception of ourselves? Jesus saw in us what we could not see in ourselves. The more his passion swelled, the more he desired to help us understand ourselves. However, much is lost, and it remains difficult to accept that we are the ones God awaits to birth the kingdom Jesus set into motion.

Far more than the rib from Adam's side, we are made in God's image and endowed with the Father's Spirit. Indeed, this does not make us equally one with God, but we cannot escape our Creator. Our choice is to accept or deny our potential. Hence, Jesus spoke of the importance of exercising our talents and all for the greater good of the kingdom. However, with so much focus on sin and paying homage to God, the human family is not on track, and the big picture of the kingdom is unseen. How we choose to apply our God-given gifts will determine the road ahead. As anyone can see, we must choose wisely.

Jesus says, "In my Father's house there are many dwelling places" (Jn 14:2). Although we can never be all that God is, we are a regal part of the Father's life. Many understand that we share in faith but rarely speak of a role to play in the Father's plan. Instead, most are waiting on God, while God, on the other hand, is waiting for us. In effect, the kingdom stalls, and its ground divides. Many agree that we are God's hands and voices in this world, but do we believe in the full meaning of being the Body of Christ? The kingdom depends on this!

I see good things manifesting in the world despite the conflict we face in every corner. However, I have to say that it appears the adversary is pushing back much harder than our faith, not in God, but in ourselves. It does not have to be this way. God intends to instill faith, not only in God but also in ourselves. That was Jesus' mission and always was and will be the Father's desire for humanity.

In retrospect, we live with the notion that the Father exists somewhere on the other side of Jesus' cross and remains at a distance. However, separation from God is not the issue. Jesus declared in the Synagogue that God with us is the fulfillment. Jesus was not changing God's story but bringing it to life!

God's plea to the Church, "I paid a great price in the blood of my Son. Why do you still persecute me," tells another side of the story concerning God with us. It's not God at a distance but rules, rhetoric, and practices that cause harm to the soul by creating a wall between people and God. Unbelievable as it may be, here is the reason for God's sorrow. God desires to engage people. Otherwise, where is love from God and love for God? Communities in the Gospel of John clearly express their experience of God who is *Love*.

Eternal Father, it was not Jesus' intention that others would perceive you as distant to us. Jesus unveiled your loving presence. On the contrary, today, you lament because countless people of God do not know the extent of your love. Is the problem so profoundly planted that they may never know?

Who are they who do not know your heart and therefore cannot see into the hearts of your children? Christians have known since the early Church's martyrs that we are vessels of your holy life. Yet, today, why are countless people repressed by rhetoric that holds back the higher truths for which Jesus lived and died?

Jesus Responds

They are the ones in fear. Fear because they see more into the darkness and less into the light. The Father's light is the answer, not the darkness, but still, they turn to remedies to satisfy the darkness. I ask for remedies flowing from light, and the darkness vanishes.

May I say then, instead of beating on sin or fallen human nature, should we focus on the Father who makes us in light? Therefore, to exercise the rule of light, contrary to the darkness?

The Father's Voice

Far more than fair! To exercise the love as my Son has shown love is the way into my heart and I am the Source of all light.

I raise the magnitude of understanding this, not for my sake, but for the sake of all good and faithful people. What is more threatening to the world's life, that we can make a difference because we are of God, or holding onto untruths? Only to look around the world, the answer is in plain sight. God gives the lyric of the Father's Well.

The Father's Well

Child of God
Go to the Well and draw a cup of water
Place it at the edge of the Well
Do you see the cup is full?
See then, that you are the cup, and

I Am the Well
I fill you with the water of my life
You say temples of the Holy Spirit
I say, indeed, you are
Of the Father's Well
Come, quench your thirst
Drink from the Well
And be satisfied.

Aligning with the Father's Heart

Yeshua Rising from the Tomb

I see the stone lifting and sun-like rays bursting forth. Showing the point of true glorification, Jesus rises in golden light, and I hear the question, "Is it to do the things of man or God?" The answer is straightforward. I did not have to respond. I only listen as Jesus continues:

The Father's Intention

At any expense, to do the things of God. I, the Son, tell you this not just from experience, but from my relationship with the Father. The tomb was not exalted because I died, but glorious because I rose triumphantly, and that is what humanity needs to know. In and through my relationship with the Father, I did not die. I rose to a new life, fresh, clean, and without harm. Life in the Father is the message of resurrection.

Churches have taken this message and used it as an icon of the Trinity. Henceforth, as the Son rises, to the Son you must pay allegiance and give your utmost respect in every way. I am not saying there is anything wrong with that, but it does not capture the breadth of the Father's intention.

The Father intended that I would set ablaze a fire in the hearts of men and women so that they would see the Father's passion burning. Here, the same love lifted me from the depths of hell and into the light of the Father's life. I say the depths of hell merely as an expression. The only hell was my experience of going through the agony of the cross.

Am I right to say that the work of our love is measured by our alignment with the Father's heart? And accordingly, our love is the God-given lever for uplifting the kingdom of God with us now.

You are laying it out in plain sight. I add that to love as I love is not my full expectation, but that you aspire to such heights. As I say throughout the Gospels, strive to 'pick up your mat and walk.' The imperative stems from the idea that you are a work in progress, and I know how difficult the path is. Do you think I am unaware of the mayhem through which the Church was conceived?

As you draw closer to my truth, I honor you by lifting you to higher places. What will be, will be about your choosing, one day, one step at a time.

When you speak of paying homage, you direct our attention to the difference between worship and love. Not that love is void of our devotion, but that your love for us is about transforming our outward expression. I wonder, then, how do you help us understand what worship means to you?

I say so because many put me in a box, and they come, and they open the box and talk to me. Then the box is closed, and they do not know how I speak to them. Misconceptions about my love cause the gap between us. They adore me, but much like an icon as opposed to a living presence. In retrospect, many continue never knowing what I ask of them. To love me is to love outside the box.

So, you are not weighing in on your triumph over sin, rather your intention is for advancing humankind through the power of the Father's love?

As a child of the Father, God wills that you should be exalted, not condemned. Free will is a powerful gift given to frail and finite humans. As such, my intention was always to encourage spiritual growth and development. Without actualizing the depth of the Father's love with you, you have little sway. The most potent force in the universe is love, entrusted to you to accomplish great things in God's name (Jn 14:12).

The vision is to help humanity see in the Son the Father's intent for all people. I was sent to open the way into the grace of the Father's heart that you would draw near to him. On the contrary, for centuries, images of God have been marred by fictional stories. Disconcerting images, precepts, and practices contradict the depth of God's love for each one. The Father is not waiting to judge. Instead, he waits for his children to rise in the truth of his passion for you. As I have shown compassion for you, so has the Father.

Through many mixed messages, you no longer know the Father or me. You have doctrines sitting in corners as though God's passion is in one corner of your life and the Father's disapproval in another. Then, what you see as a dubious deed will determine the corner where you will find God. Hence, sometimes you foresee the Father against you and other times for you. I tell you he is always for you!

Although I aspire to awaken you to the full passion of the Father, to wake up to that truth is still up to you. Heaven does not await you, and neither does hell. I am here for you now, so too is heaven. You enter when unveiling the passion that already lives within you. For many, this could be a long road, while only a door to open for others. I am not judging this!

You have the gift of free will. How the Father brings all things to completion is affected by the exercise of your free will. You know now that I am talking about choices and actions motivated by love and compassion. Be not afraid of the Father, rather, exercise the love that shaped you from the beginning.

When you say that the Father is always for us, you affirm that God's genius is for supporting the greatest good in all and for all. If so, the idea may be confusing for some because many quickly shy away from you for the littlest things. Are you saying you may disapprove of an action that runs against the grain of your love but never the person?

Your point of reference is understandable. I add that my love is unconditional and non-judgmental. Contrarily, my call is to move my people forward, not by force or fear but by my love for them.

You talk about old precepts and practices that injure but give no examples while I can think of many. What reason have you?

Because the churches are not all wrong, but that history has altered the foundation of my truth. Many with ears to hear will agree. No need to point fingers, but to reveal God's heart.

Jesus, you say, "As children of the Father, God wills that we should be exalted, not condemned." Have we raised the bar so high in your name that we do not understand? Or have we blundered to know your life and mission?

In retrospect, you have done both. The questions point to the fundamentals of this book. You have all that you need to do 'greater works' than I. However, most do not understand, because my underlying message did not filter into your growth and development. Look again at the dichotomies of Paul. They tell the story.

Although you have addressed this, please be patient when I raise the question once again. Concerning the idea of living life to the fullest, many say that we are here not to go through all the trials and tribulations, but to live life in joy. How do you respond?

Of course, there is much truth to this; the confusion concerns a person's perception of joy. For the most part, humankind has turned to money and material things as their source of happiness. Although it may look like joy on the outside, the story differs if you look at the soul's life. Unfortunately, many strive for freedom and happiness on that basis.

On this ground, Wall Street is the muscle of America, as though an icon of my premise, but only I am the way and the truth. Although it may look like success for those who pump it up, I say not.

The Father Intervenes

I am the muscle of the world. Your joy is in me. Holistically working together is the work of the kingdom, and if you are not, I cannot allow this to continue. I do not place judgment on this, nor do I condemn it. However, creation is for a highly profound reason, and the human family must do their part. According to my plan, humanity is not fulfilling it because, without just cause, many are not sharing in life's joy. Many suffer health and financial hardships and more. The angst should not be to the extent that I see.

Here, I am not talking about merely giving to the poor. I am talking about putting your love for God before all things. People fear that language, primarily because of the misunderstanding and interpretations through the many centuries. To put God first is the true road to happiness, not boredom but joy, not lack but abundance.

For a good reason, in my image, you exist, but you must use your God-given gifts to find me in the mix of your life. Find me in the talents that you have; find me in the loved ones that surround you and realize who you are and why you are here. Lest you are swallowed up in the wrong idea of joy. I say so because greed is consuming the world, and it pains me to see. In my view, this is not joyful any more than for my Son.

Is it fair to ask about cures withheld for monetary gains? Would this be an example of things you refer to when saying people are in angst without just cause?

It makes no sense to see the withholding of that which is beneficial to humanity's greater good. Those who withhold live in fear and do not consider the prospect of my giving. Give in the name of my love, and you will have more than mere monetary profits.

And yes! Your example is in the realm of things I speak of, sadly, the list is much longer than I care to say.

Indeed, we have lost sight of the things of God. We weigh heavily on practices of prayer and retribution and less on the higher gifts for transforming the world. We talk about good deeds but place them in boxes less to transform one's soul. We have learned to walk a road of doings and less a way of being. Yet, you laid down the ground of the Father's love for being light to the world. It scares me to think how much time has passed, and are we too late?

Dear one, I would not have you spend your years to say yes, it is too late. No! My love is not so shallow. May those who have ears hear the weight of this dialogue.

Jesus, why have you chosen the title *Yeshua* for this vision?

I do not want readers to forget my heritage as a Jew. *Yeshua* is an honored title, and my legacy as a Jew was a choice and an honor. I do not judge or differentiate. Many paths lead to the Father. But, to understand the depth of God's love may not be as quickly defined. I did not intend to fight against the Old Tradition but to open a door, and many to this day, peek in and see the truth in me.

Light Bearers of the Kingdom

Jesus' Limp Body

Released from the nails, Jesus slumps over while cradling the crown of thorns in his arms. He is lifeless and the cross crude and oppressing, a vision without grace, exuding anguish, and sorrow. Gently, they cradle the limp corpse. Jesus narrates:

Warriors of the Father's Light

> Dark, graceless, strained, dry, empty, lifeless, speechless, numb, null, I have no words to describe that moment of realizing the transition from a full life in the flesh to a corpse. Like a light bulb going out, the darkness filled me as though emptying a room.
>
> Then the Father breathed into me, and I came to life, or you could say to light again. Such is the power of life within all people. All children are of the Father's Spirit. This light I saw in them, some more brightly than others. The kingdom of God hinges on the quotient of light that you unfold. And, if faint, it cannot shine on the Father's kingdom. The brighter your heart, the more the kingdom unveils through you.

You have thought for centuries that the kingdom of God is a house that God built up in the sky. You think you are helpless as children depending on him to save you and bring you back into 'Paradise Lost.' But I tell you that is not true. The kingdom is far from static by nature.

When you step onto this world and come to light or life, the same is for you as for me. You are born into this world with the Father's radiance, and that light is the kingdom within you. And bringing the Father's light into the darkness of this world has always been your work. We know it can be like an obstacle course when sent forth into this world – however, the purpose of life is extraordinarily profound.

I never said that it would be easy. If anything, I demonstrate that life is not painless. We are aware of the many stories that talk about God and creation – how man sinned and was then thrust into the toil of survival. Many truths exist within the telling of this story, but also many falsehoods.

Because the matter of concern is in-depth, I do not find it necessary to tell every little detail of the Father's plan for the world. But you must realize that you are light, and you are far more than 'fallen.' You are the Father's warriors of light to bring light into a place that it has never been before.

Now, I am not talking about the sunlight. The sunlight is for your well-being. I am talking about the light of our Father's life, fueled by the most potent force in the universe. That is why you are here, i.e., to fill this place with love. The earth has little meaning without the love that you bring. When the world brings forth more decay than love, it cannot be. What I ask of you is to be a warrior of the Father's light.

I came to open a door for those who would realize the gift within themselves. Desiring them to see the light of God as the sunshine that flows from within them was my mission. As I spoke my truth, the light was so intense to penetrate the souls of those listening. At times even for you, my light is known to pull you through demanding situations.

Your foremost responsibility was always to bring light to the land you know as earth. Carefully prepared by the Father's breath, creation is miraculous in and of itself. However, you must till its soil, each one according to one's abilities. You must cultivate and create the world you seek through your goodness and give it meaning and integrity.

Jesus words are humbling. As I write, they often bring me to my knees. Here, I pause to process what is hard to express in the written word.

Returning much later, I lament: Beloved Jesus, I tremble to see you holding the crown of thorns in your hands.

The crown represents my victory. I hold it in my arms not as a sign of defeat but quite the contrary. The brute of humans cannot take away the Father's light.

How am I to understand that you see the crown of thorns as a symbol of your light?

Those who attempted to mark me did so with the crown of thorns. I did not reject their insults. Instead, triumphantly, I display the crown to illustrate how small their insults are compared to the royalty of the Father's Temple.

Though the Father's call is to all, he is not anticipating all to participate. God understands the difficulty in the road ahead, but do not forget the Father sees triumph in each one's success. I would tell my congregation that if they could see what God sees, they would walk the uncertain road again and again. Somehow, I knew this in my heart.

Although we cannot see what God ultimately sees, one can develop a sense of God's presence. After all, life can befuddle the best minds, and without faith, one sees only an empty road ahead. On the other hand, through faith, one may encounter God's grace within all things. And who would not wish to say yes to all of it?

Talent shows overwhelm the span of television networks. How often the panelists will express to a talented contestant, "I want to see it all." How much more do you wish to experience God's infinite path of life and discovery?

Jesus says, "The brighter your heart, the more the kingdom unveils through you." What makes your heart burn bright is aligning with the Father's love. How you align is not so hard to understand but often harder to set into motion. First, there is the matter of believing that you are a precious child of the Father. Without the Spirit of God, you would have no life.

But this alone does not cause your heart and soul to burn bright. As you discover and unfold the experience of God with you, then the inner flame burns brighter. As you allow the divine presence to lead the way, you walk a path aligning with the soul's purpose.

As already stated, it is not difficult to understand, but at times it's challenging to find one's way. God calls some to choose what may look contrary to this world's direction, although not to the dissatisfaction of one's highest purpose. According to one's gifts, each soul walks a unique path. For this reason, Jesus talks about exercising one's talents for the highest good, and nothing stands taller than the kingdom Jesus proclaimed. To do so is what Jesus means when naming you "warriors of the Father's light." When aligning your giftedness with the Father, you become the fire of the kingdom. To be light bearers of God's kingdom is to carry the Father's Spirit in word and deed, and here the kingdom shines through you.

Many strive to gain a sense of their value before God through external acts. Although there is nothing wrong with that, many never step into the light. Yet, God does not wait for you to complete a process but to wholeheartedly step onto the path of the Father's light just as you are. And that's when the miracles begin. In truth, God denies no one. We deny ourselves.

Precious Mysteries in Jesus' Words

> The Father's children are like seashells in the sand. People walk along the shore to pick the finest and most pleasing of shells. They collect them and adore them and enjoy filling their homes with the nostalgia of the sea.
>
> And so, with God's children, they make of themselves the most beautiful shells to house the Father's Spirit, and the Father welcomes them and fills his home with the awe of their beautiful souls. Oh! He does not collect them as showpieces to put on a shelf but holds them close to his heart.

Avenue of Abundance

Well-Proportioned Oak Tree

In a bit of wind about life's challenges, my ruminating pauses, and the Father reminds me to trust that he "has a plan and to be well." With the tone set, the showing of a tall and well-proportioned oak tree towers over me. Standing alone in a vast meadow, it soars high into the horizon, an oasis of its own accord. Displaying strong branches, buds, and blossoms, rich in color and design, I experience ecstasy within a garden of majestic proportions. Drawing closer, what looked from a distance a barren place, the revelation of its soothing beauty pours through me.

Directing me further, the Father calls my attention to the colorful birds that fill its many branches. And then to see the squirrels playing around its trunk and climbing through the limbs alongside many life forms: leisurely snails, jumping rabbits, and skipping chipmunks feed on the acorns. All reside safely within the grand tree's shelter, food, and respite offerings. Through the Father's voice, the connection between service and abundance unfolds:

Lack has No Place in the Kingdom

For years upon years, the tree thrives, not merely surviving but thriving with life! For many, it provides food and shelter, whether from the winds, storms, or predators. As you can see, the list goes on. Nevertheless, as you already understand, the point to be made lies within the question of service.

Service is an avenue of abundance, not a channel for lack and self-incrimination. For centuries your thinking has confused the idea of kindness and selflessness as working hand in hand. Subsequently, many fear the obligation to give even the shirt off their backs or to surrender treasured gifts. Service is not a road to poverty, nor a path into selflessness. On the contrary, the way is too abundance!

Be sure that you are not intended to live disproportionately, but that what you give is returned to you twofold, threefold, and more. However, the act is not just 'giving' to gain but giving because there is joy in the giving and joy in the flurry of life that you serve. Is that not the greater reward? You know what I say here, and that is not to deny your own needs. Indeed, in manifold ways, I will meet them, and you will not suffer lack.

Lack has no place in the kingdom. So, it stands that if one is living in 'lack,' one has not stepped foot onto the ground of the kingdom. The kingdom of God is about the disposition of one's heart where true happiness exists. In your heart, I sit with you! Selfish gain has no place where I sit.

Do you ever wonder why you have complete satisfaction when you give a helping hand to make someone's day? Such gratification is because the substance of the kingdom is at play with you. Some have many things, and their banks are full, but their hearts are empty. If they continue to rely on what is outside of them, they will not know true happiness. A path of selfishness and greed will never satisfy for I am God, and I have made you in my image, and to all, I am in service.

My Son has reflected the depth of my service in the complete giving of his life. And he sends his followers also to serve in my name. I am infinite. I am everything, and I am here for you, and I have everything to give in every way. I thrive and live among my children.

People do not see that my intention is not to hide from them but to rise within them. Hear then, why the visions in this writing are essential. Wake up, children! I am with you! Wake up to my hand upon you! Recognize my presence! Believe that in your heart I reside, and you will watch the magic in your life!

Service to others is not necessarily about giving to the poor or 'giving the shirt off one's back,' far more, a way of life! It may be as simple as a smile. The disposition is one of honesty and integrity. Service is about being truthful, responsible, and understanding. Service is an attitude aligned with the Father's goodwill for all. Far from a fluffy love, it is a regal attitude of doing the right thing for the greater good of all and all things.

When the Father says, "Lack has no place in the kingdom," he proclaims service is an avenue of abundance. Interestingly, Jesus says, "What you do to another, you do to me. And what you do for another, you do for me." And he explicitly spells out the example of giving a cup of water to someone thirsty. The teachings are profound directives about what it means to love while something extraordinary is at play beneath the surface.

Here, a new dimension of understanding unfolds to us. I pause for a breath to allow it to sink in, then I ask, Father, what have you to say when it comes to living in abundance?

> The wisdom you seek unfolds as you explore the truth of my proximity to people. However, beneath the surface, you say to yourself that the scope and meaning will eventually come to light, and no one can deny it.
>
> On the other hand, people agree that life is not a mystery to solve but a mystery to live. However, that does not mean all roads are wide open. Instead, there exists a most prominent way to live the enigma. The most fruitful path is to live within the realm of my love! And my love is an avenue of infinite possibilities.

Regarding what is extraordinary and lies beneath the surface, Father, you are everything and have everything to give. Hence, abundance has an interior dimension rarely discussed. The visions illustrate the depth of your good intentions. I am talking primarily about the idea that you do not create a divide between God and humans. Your love is not divisive but a magnificent two-way street. The choice is ours whether we are to live in the profundity of your love or not.

The Scriptures tell many stories about Jesus directing believers to pick up their mats and walk. Father, have we lost one of the most precious gifts of the Son?

I, the Father, choose to love my creation. Although less a conscious choice for me, it is my only choice from beginning to end because that is who I am. Of course, I could choose otherwise, but that would defy who I am and the creation I love. I say so for those whose doubt still lingers. That is the residue of ages of misunderstanding,

To answer your question. It is written that no greater love exists than to lay down one's life for a friend. Does that not say enough to see how precious the gift is that is not recognized? What did you hear in the sound of my plea?

For all eternity, I cannot imagine your plea escaping my soul. Indeed, you have honored me with an indelible mark that is eternally etched on my heart by the most profound sorrow and a passion running deeper. The throes of your heart's desire and pain rapture me. My tears say one thing and my soul another. Beyond words, I am forever grateful for the gift of your favor to be so close to your heart, and to honor you with a voice so small brings me eternally to my knees.

You cannot and will not be eternally on your knees.
Nay! You will be eternally by my side!

Indeed, I must step away to return later–much later. I cannot proceed with my heart so heavy with love overflowing.

Pick Up Your Mat

How many followers did Jesus transform with the gift of his divine love? He teaches us to build the kingdom, profound in word and deed. Jesus was a teacher and the kingdom his lesson. Untiringly, he taught his followers how to pick each other up. The kingdom depended on that because to do so was at the center of the Father's heart. And that has never changed.

When I speak of the corridor opening before me to peer into a new dimension of abundance. I turn to the actions of Jesus when telling his people to pick themselves up and walk. Far more than healing their bodies, he was healing their souls' lack of love. And he could only raise them up through the power of the Father's love at work in him.

Because Jesus' approach is essential to our soul's well-being, we can no longer deny the comingling of the human and divine. Because at the heart of it, this is our most significant source of abundance. However, so many are lacking emotionally and spiritually because they do not believe in the power of God's Spirit with them. Instead, they turn to outward practices and figures of authority.

Jesus helped his followers to see who they were in God's eyes and the love that filled them. Above all else, he knew how to heal the human heart, which was central to his mission.

This reaches into the enigma that God was speaking of earlier about "living in the enigma of God's love" that cannot be defined. However, a power with us and becomes stronger the more we align with the gift and exercise of God's love. Hence, the impetus for realizing transformation.

Actualizing the love already with us, is no different than the man who found the treasure in the field and sold everything he had for it. Nothing can possibly compare! Do you believe in the joy, abundance, and divine assurances? No ground can compete!

I talk about the magic that happens when people go out of their way to help someone, and the gratification is more than money can buy. Such cases signify that beneath the giving, the more significant portion is the healing of a soul. Here identifies a contact point of the kingdom that Jesus unveils. In effect, like a cup of water given to the Father, who gives back to the giver.

Father, when you speak of the "enigma," do you refer to the active commingling of the human and divine?

> Dear messenger, you speak my truth. That is why I say
> my love is the ground on which to stand, as you know.
> And then to see the holy ground on which you stand is
> indeed holy because I stand with you.

The tenet profoundly speaks of the kingdom's essence and depends on us to bring it to completion.

> The missing link to the kingdom is to know the ground
> on which you walk is holy because I reside within. For
> those who realize, the kingdom comes.

So, as we recognize your Spirit in and with us, the potential of the kingdom comes? The precept reveals the kingdom's household, not people chosen by you, but those who willfully embrace the essence of your invitation. Hence, Jesus' parable of those invited to the wedding feast.

> Indeed, acknowledging the kingdom's work is essential.
> There are no sects, some chosen and others not; all is in
> your hands, and I am with all. The theory is not

complicated but has become complex through the differences you have created.

What will it take for your people to act on the kingdom as you see it?

It matters not where people position in faith but accepting one another in the name of my love. Hence, the layout of this book.

So, on varying levels, you say that churches have learned to defend their truth and, therefore, to sequester themselves according to rules cast from fears.

Indeed, although the process is infinitely complex, it does not have to be. A change is coming, and I want my children to understand what it means to be on board. Hence, my intention from the day I called you!

Although it is a mystery, I see a complete picture.

Yes! However, the avenues are multidimensional and not limited by human reasoning. No matter the complexity, I am always the way because I am the ground of all life and love.

Some people of good faith work more from models that this entire book captures as weak foundations. When praying, they look externally to good jobs, beautiful cars, homes, and the list continues. These are appearances of abundance, but they are not what I see as such. They are what the mind sees. I am sitting within the recesses of your souls, not your heads.

Do not be put off by what I say. I respond in ways intended to bring people closer to the wisdom of their souls. I lead them to higher places. If I answered all according to the flow of their prayers, I would falsely lead people through a material walk in life, which is not my goal. I make you in my image!

I know the desire of one's soul, and sometimes not all is as it seems. Often, those who appear to have the least serve higher purposes than those who appear to have the most.

I have only scratched the surface here, for you to know that although I have a place with each one, you have a choice to align with your highest good or the workings of the mind. When aligning with me, the path is for the highest outcome beginning with yours. Countless churches lean on human reasoning, and the kingdom is not evident. As I am in loving service, so too is my call.

People you see suffering reflect the sad failure to establish the truth of my kingdom. And some think it is best to leave those suffering to themselves. Such thinking is the cause for casting my children out of the garden, not me. My intention is for you, my children, to build the kingdom. The choice is at your doorstep.

When God identifies peoples' suffering with humanity's failure to exercise the truth of the kingdom, he is opening our eyes. Consequently, human suffering has multiple faces that present a complexity of challenges; some cases are vast in scale, and others small. So also, are the extent of reasons for people to shy away from the problems.

God knows the size and complexity of the issues we are facing. Here, the Creator is helping us see through God's eyes that it is not about how much we can do but doing what we can do, which makes a difference. By doing so, hope rises through us. Hope is not something on a shelf waiting for us to discover, but God's action exercised through us.

I note that Jesus was hands-on when delivering exceeding love and hope flowing from the Father. Accordingly, might I say this gets at the heart of living in abundance.

> You are not wrong to say so. Although you must know, the process is challenging for you to grasp. I wish to add that my kindness tempers my patience. Many lessons within these visions may be hard for some to consume, but the treasures will speak for themselves.

I think how often I am bewildered by the problem of corporate giants across the globe dominating the world and working less from the heart and more from greed. And they are successfully doing so!

> I guess you have not looked out your window lately. What do you see? Does the world look as though it is in a successful cycle? That is interesting because, from my view, every 'man for himself' is a complete failure.

I understand your expression, but how are we to change this dilemma?

Who said you had to change it? The only thing you must do is align with my vision for realizing your God-given potential. And it would be better to use it for the highest good, and change will override.

According to good intentions, we have grown to believe that sacrifice and fasting intend to earn the benefit of God's favor. As I understand, much of this relates to Jesus' sacrifice. How does or does this not benefit a greater good?

In today's world, the idea of sacrifice and fasting is far more superficial than the action of one's soul. In their highest form, sacrifices spring from the soul to move oneself, another, or even a situation. To reach extended heights in prayer is not only by fasting but by fasting with the right intentions.

Those who fast because they are told do not necessarily achieve a higher form of prayer but more often procure external acts. I wish people to acknowledge the inner life of their souls. Instead, they turn to outward appearances as opposed to the treasure of my presence.

Would you say this is partly due to the fears born from our poor understanding of selfless service in God's name?

Indeed, I am not a selfless God. Love is not selfless. Why would I place that demand on you who are of my image? I give all and desire all to receive all. And I do not provide to reap the rewards but to satisfy love. If my children do not see or respond adversely, what is there to receive, for them, or me? The world is working through this, and I am watching. My children, who seek the greater good for all, stand out. On this ground, fear has no place, yet it is shaking the earth.

So, to give is not a question of denying one's needs but a question of balance.

Love will sometimes give beyond measure, but never from fear. Fear is the danger and the cause of much confusion and misunderstanding, so the question is one of fear or love. I Am *Love* and move my people only from a posture of love.

Would you say people are not in touch with their fears?

Being out of touch is a sad situation. Humanity has emphasized falsely from the intellect even in my name for centuries. In the process, people are out of touch with themselves. My wish for this work is to open a door for getting in touch. The world is experiencing a rapid change that urges you to get in touch!

What did Jesus say or do to help people in this regard?

The point is critical because Christianity has understood his cross as a means for people to reconnect to me, and less with themselves. I am not outside of you but within, and fear has no gain with me any more than it does for you. My Son came to let it be known that I am Father, and in all that he said and did, he demonstrated my love, not my punishment and condemnation. I am the antithesis of fear.

Sadly, I have talked with many, and still, they have difficulty accepting the posture of your love for them. They are more in touch with their unworthiness and bow instead for your mercy.

I know the crowds to which you refer. They are lost to old reasoning. Hence, I give you the heading: Resurrecting Jesus' Truth!

The Father's Throne

Heart to Heart

After laying back and snuggling into my bed, a hypnotic ray of energy gently streamed down on me. The cascading hues of red spiraling downward were evenly matched by spiraling shades of blue flowing upward from me. My focus shifted directly to my heart space. In a moment of complete ecstasy, I wondered about the meaning of this profound connection. Then expanding outwards as they rise, the colorful tones fade while swirling higher and higher until dissipating into the ethers. In its wake, a vortex opens. Jesus explains:

The Father's Bosom

> I open your eyes to the Father's connection with you and with each individual on the earth. Divine communication spans far beyond the grasp of human reason. Because of your difficulty understanding the proximities of space in relation to God, you do not know how God communicates God's self. And, to each one, the Father makes a home. The melding of the human and divine is not so easy to explain, but the reality is that each one is in communion with the Father.

You have a share in God's life to the extent of which is in your hands. Do you see the potential each one carries? A God connection that is real and energetic.

Many believe, God is separate from the earth. Conversely, all that exists is embodied in the energy of the Father within his bosom. Do you see how tender and loving this image is? Real to life, yet more people live in fear of the Father than not!

I came to break such binders, at least to start a tear in the fabric of humanity's fears. However, this is not what is mirroring back to us. We wish to rejuvenate the earth and humankind. The anxiety must lift, so that people may see again who they are and to whom they belong. They are children of the Father, and their life exists in the bosom of the Father. Yet, how high are the numbers who feel they are in exile?

I came that people would rise from the grip of fear and all its damages to them that they would celebrate the true picture of a God who embraces them. As you see, what I have accomplished has dwindled over the centuries. Recall the stories told about passing a message from one to another. By the time it gets to the end of the line, the story is hardly recognizable. My truth is no different.

For those who hear, I am with you not half-heartedly, but wholeheartedly just as you are. You must see that in God's eyes, you are much more than what you have believed yourself to be. Come out of the dark and come into the light that your eyes may open. Let the light of the Son shower you so that you may see again the fire that burns within. During these unprecedented times, can you see the importance?

Here, Jesus illustrates the ground of the Father's love collectively and individually revealing the depths of God with us. Jesus speaks to many who are confused and stuck in a century's old language. Unfortunately, over the course of time misunderstanding has closed uncountable doors on God's love. I often hear that people are to blame for God's rejection and the misfortune about the way of things today.

Indeed, there is some merit to the allegations. However, the remedies available are not viable. If Jesus were with us today, do you think he could make a difference? People are seeing that love is the way and fear is the enemy. Church history is a testament to the victories of fear and its incomprehensible devastation. This fear isn't merely an imbalance, but for centuries, it has gone off the charts. Fear has many faces, although nothing is more debilitating than the fear of God's rejection. The blow is to the life of the soul and the graces of the Father—the very thing that drives the Father's plea.

Do you see why Jesus came in the Father's name? Not to die for sin, but to breathe life into people's souls and drive our worst enemy away. And the timeless plea of the Father continues; still, the enemy is at work. And the fear of God, the ghost of centuries, sitting on the hearts of countless people, and the Father's plea falling on deaf ears. So, Jesus says, "...blessed are they who have ears to hear."

I do not seek to create more unrest but to render God's truth for granting freedom and peace to those trapped in the centuries of untruths born from fear. God's throne exists within every man and woman's heart for which no man has dominion. Jesus teaches divine love, not divine authority. Again, Jesus' "yoke" is easy because his "yoke" was, is, and will forever be "love." He willed not to lord over anyone but to freely guide people into the place of the Father's heart. If not welcomed, then Jesus told his apostles "…to shake the dust off their heels."

The "Heart Vortex," like the kingdom, is God with us and cannot be seen, although experienced, and that is the nature of the connection Jesus unveils. God's throne is not in buildings or words but a magnificent seat within the hearts of men and women. Hence, the inner dwelling ought not to be denied but celebrated!

Through Jesus' life and teachings, one may see God is not the one to hold anyone away. As with the Father's words, "I paid a great price in the blood of my Son. Why do you still persecute me?" After two thousand years, my hand shivers to think of who, when, and why. For centuries, the Father's voice in silence is not the sound of wrath but patience and care when approaching human fragility.

Many good and faithful people understand the heart of God, but not all understand the Father's throne. Jesus did not claim the Father's throne. Instead, he showed the way to the Father's heart. He was not looking for a place of honor, but to honor the Father; that was his mission. Personifying the intensity of God's heart was his highest expression of the kingdom he proclaimed. And where would we be today if he failed to love?

One must ask if our salvation is so static that it takes the blood of Christ to save us. Or that we are dynamically and vibrantly made for sharing intimately in the saving love of the Father who creates us? For that reason, Jesus came in the Father's name and died in his name. Our salvation is not about the afterlife but the strength of God's incomprehensible love for us and the greater purpose of creating heaven on earth. We are far more than fallen, but temples of God's life forged in the image of God. And according to Jesus, we have all we need to bring it forward.

I turn again to the announcement of Jesus' mission as he read from the scriptures to proclaim that he is anointed by the Father to bring "Good News" (Lk 4:18-21). Publicly, he trumpeted the release of those held captive, recovery of sight to the blind, and liberation for the oppressed. Then, bringing the declarations under one umbrella, he declared a time of God's favor. And then adding that the scriptures are fulfilled in their hearing. Again, after highlighting six pivotal points, Jesus' mission begins, and a new paradigm unfolds:

Anointed by the Father

Throughout the scriptures, Jesus demonstrated the anointing of the Father. How many miracles? How many thousands drew near to his side? How much love?

Good News for the Poor

What news is more valuable and life-giving to the poor than unveiling the extent of the Father's love whose favor is not for altar sacrifice or purchase with copper, silver, or gold?

Release for the Captives

What is more life-giving to those held captive by the heavy burdens of the law than to hear the "Good News" of a loving Father? Jesus did not only teach the love of God but demonstrated God is *Love*. His approach liberated those weighed down by heavy loads. He declared his yoke is easy because the Father's yoke is love.

Recovery of Sight to the Blind

Jesus brought sight to the blind by opening the eyes of faith to all who could not see the blessings of an intimately loving Father.

Liberation of the Oppressed

What is more liberating for those oppressed by the fear of God's wrath and punishment than unveiling the hope in an unconditionally loving God?

Year of the Lord's Favor

Jesus proclaimed a time of God's favor. He demonstrated the good news of God's kingdom, not only in parables but in the love of God he exemplified.

The Scripture is Fulfilled in Your Hearing

"In your hearing, this scripture is fulfilled." Jesus was not only about words but manifesting the Father's divine love and presence with them. Here, Jesus revealed the ground of the kingdom for those who have ears to hear. And to be sure, if you can, try to understand the weight of misunderstanding God during Jesus' time. Our ancestors were in darkness, given the many misconceptions of an angry and wrathful God; and perpetuated by laws that held them tightly in the grips of fear. And so, Jesus announced, "Today, this scripture is fulfilled."

PART 6

The End Time

A New Beginning

Handing Down the Light

Two Burning Flames

In this vision, Jesus takes the lead with a gentle and ceremonial approach. He begins: "This day, I give you a new image. Here you see, I hold out my palms to you."

Before me, he stands with palms reaching out and a fire intensely burning in each hand. The flames are so bright I cannot see clearly, but the beauty of their light reflecting off Jesus' face. I perceive them as blazing candles with the brilliance of the sun glowing from his palms. Jesus continues:

The Father's Flame

> Yes, you are right to say so, but there are no candles. There are two flames. In my left hand, I carry the flame of light to the world, and in my right hand, I carry a flame to pass on to those that will hear my word, and they will take that flame into their hearts.
>
> I give you the true image of the Son who came to light a fire in the hearts of men and women that the Father's light would be set ablaze. And on this fire, so many leaders throughout the centuries have continued to throw their unclean water. I announce this fire burns now, and it has never been hotter.

For those who hear my word, I the Christed one, pass on this flame to you. As on the day I stood in the Synagogue to read and I concluded '…in your hearing, this scripture is fulfilled.' At that moment, I passed on the flame of the Father's love to those who would hear. As the flame reflected in my followers' hearts, they saw in themselves the light of the kingdom.

Today, you have some who are beginning to see that the kingdom lives within. And I say, it took two thousand years to realize this because my truth did not pass on, as I passed it onto my followers. For centuries, it was washed away, daggered, pruned, and torched. And it was not the way I wished for it to burn. Even so, the ashes remained enough that they could not wash away the full impact of my message.

My light burned strongly in those following me. Here, I refer again to the lives of the martyrs. The strength in them burned brighter and more durable than that of lions. Not that they could devour the lion, but that they could stand before the lion without fear. Not even lions can stand without fear when they are cornered and facing death.

Must you wonder why they wished to stamp out the perceived threat? They could not understand their strength. Instead, overwhelmed by a power they feared would overcome them.

Following the loss of my truth, many wished to lead for vain glory and greed, which continued through the centuries, and here you are today – many churches touting the 'Day of Judgment' with the sheep to the right and the goats to the left. I tell you none of that is here.

This ideology is much like the Old Testament when I stood on trial before the Pharisees. And today, I am asking you to tell me please who are the goats and who are the sheep? I would rather that you see what burns in your heart. Does it burn with the flame of the Father's love, or is it more like burnt ashes?

Are you still running from your sins or trying to fix them, or are you living in the light? Do you know how to live in the light? Do you know how to stop judging one another, because the more you look at sin as the problem, the more you judge? Look to the light, and the more you love. Do you see what is missing? If you do not see what is missing now, you never will.

Jesus' momentum was always about how we make a home of ourselves for God, and never about God's judgment, punishment, or even our sins. The perception is a far reach from our ancestors' perceptions of sin and judgment. I recall that Jesus made an unforgettable impression, however, clouded by a strained history.

Beloved Jesus, throughout the pages, much is said about "being without fear." I understand, but something more needs to be said about the meaning. Sometimes, I am afraid of inevitable consequences or what others may say or do. Nonetheless, I do not shrink but stand firm in my truth as it is rooted in your love. What is the difference when feeling afraid and being strong in heart?

To be without fear does not necessarily mean to be unafraid. Instead, to have the courage to face your fears and God's love is the courage to stand and face them courageously.

As we understand, this explains your prayer to the Father during your agony in the garden. The martyrs were afraid. However, what held them firmly was love mightier than fear of the enemy's egregious and shameless acts against them.

It's Up to You

The Locust's

Seeing the locust's big, bulging red eyes creeping into view, I know precisely the meaning that stares back at me. Partly enchanting and partly bewitching, I wish to escape. Yet, knowing there is nowhere to turn, I am still. As though the clock stops and the Father begins:

> I Am that I Am, and I Am among my people. Although you may think so, my prophets did not leave the planet long ago. Listen to this writing, and hear my truth unfold, and let your heart be the measure of my voice.
>
> During this critical time, my hand reaches out to you. I am giving you this gift, but you must listen. The energy is intense. It will pull you left or right. You read in the scriptures about the coming of judgment, but do not misunderstand. Judgment is not by my hands, rather by yours.
>
> Already, we see the divide among you. I am asking you to make the right choices for your soul and your world. Be guided by my divine wisdom within you. I did not make all my children scholars so that they would know me. I give you a heart and a soul that responds to my truth. I am the Maker, find refuge in me, and make time to realize the choices are yours. I will give you

strength. You should know that you are my sons and daughters. However, you are not one with me if your heart is at a distance.

I do not want you to put me in a box and then place me on a shelf. I am asking you to choose 'All that is' because I Am everything. Choose wisely, wherefore it's easy to be lost when hanging onto the ideals of men and women. During these stressful times, see through the darkness and see me watching over you.

Father, in the scriptures, Jesus said, "…no one knows the day or the hour," and although we do not know, your mercy and compassion reach out to those who hear. Would you please explain more?

Already, I have given much to those who listen. I will say, not by fear, that I reveal the depths of my heart but from love. There is time. People know that the world is changing; how it will change is in your hands.

Is it better to view the coming days, months, and years less as an end, and more as a new beginning?

With me, it is not the end, but always a new beginning for those who listen. Although it may not be an end for those who do not, it will bear its consequences. You cannot hurtle over the line at the last minute as an Olympic pole-vaulter. You are either prepared or not.

The Power of God's Intention

In the past two decades, we have read an awful lot about the power of our intention. Then, the idea slowly lost steam. On a different note, we have heard little to nothing about the power of God's intention. The reality is: little power in our intentions exists if they are not aligned with God's. To explain, I begin by revisiting the moment when Jesus read in the Synagogue. He stood up to read from the scroll of the Prophet Isaiah, and by choice, Jesus turned to this passage:

> The Spirit of the Lord is upon me,
> because he has anointed me
> to bring good news to the poor.
> He has sent me to proclaim release to the captives
> and recovery of sight to the blind,
> to let the oppressed, go free,
> to proclaim the year of the Lord's favor. (Lk 4:18-19)

Jesus sat down to conclude, "today in your hearing, this Scripture is fulfilled." The event was not just about Jesus, especially since Jesus was not just about Jesus. Instead, the reading exudes revelations about God's intentions. Here, there is nothing to say about commands, such as do's and don'ts, if's, and's or but's, or threats to tout! On the contrary, the time of God's favor was fully revealed in Jesus' words founded on the truth of the Father's love and intentions for humanity.

Jesus also added that blessed are they who have ears to hear. What have we been hearing for two thousand years? Our eyes are closed, and ears blocked to the truth Jesus unveils. Hence, the reason he reveals six grueling visions about the destruction of his truth and why we do not have the profundity of his declaration.

He is sent to usher forth a new paradigm founded on the Father who is before him. His words are misunderstood within the context of a tradition that played its part to hold God's people bound to sin and fear of God. The paradigm Jesus ushered forth did not die on the cross. It died in the hearts of men and women. God calls us to resurrect Jesus' truth, and those who have ears to hear will do it!

I lament that we have understood God's will more as repressing and less intending for us a joyous life. Yet, Jesus declared the time of God's favor, and throughout his life, he revealed images of the kingdom. However, consumed by the problem of sin, we have not seen or heard the true intention of God or the voice of the Son.

Instead, we interpret his saving actions as lifting us out of the darkness of human sinfulness. Yet, how many fail to feel wholly pleasing to God? Jesus said, "My yoke is easy," because weighing on peoples' hearts was never God's intention—not then any more than now—but to open the corridor to the Father's heart. However, it's not a corridor leading to somewhere outside of time. Instead, within the recesses of one's soul exists the *Love* we seek and the ground for "being in time" now!

The Father's Voice

> I give you myself. I am with you. Carry me in time and know that you hold me within, and that is my choice. I wait for you to see and embrace me.

I think of how often I misplace my car keys. Baffled, I search everywhere, and hours are wasted only to find they have been hanging from my belt strap the entire time. The "keys" to the kingdom Jesus proclaimed are not left for Peter to decide, but they have always been with us. Safely placed within each soul, the Father patiently waits for us to unlock the door.

We have not understood that the ground on which we walk is holy by virtue of who we are, and *Creation* waits for us still to step out of the darkness and into the light that we are. The corridor Jesus opens is one of aligning with the truth of God with us now! Would a good Father wish anything less for his sacred vessels than a life showered by the abundance of his blessings? In the Gospel of Luke Jesus asks:

> Is there anyone among you who, if your child asks for a fish, will give a snake instead of a fish? Or if the child asks for an egg, will give a scorpion? If you then, who are evil, know how to give good gifts to your children, how much more will the heavenly Father give the Holy Spirit to those who ask him! (Lk 11:11-13)

Why do so many shy away from the Father? Recall his opening words at the start of this book:

> I do not lord over my children like a king collecting taxes and filling his purses. No! Yet, you approach me

as though you owe me something and are not paying up! You do not know my love for you! I am not blaming anyone. However, the time now is to wake up to the truth of my desire for *Creation*, not my displeasure. For centuries humanity has been waiting on me. While on the contrary, I have been waiting for you to wake up to me!

God desires that we live in his light, not the fear of God's judgment. Our Maker is not distant; that is our doing. The time to rise is now, and the signs are everywhere. If you believe the world is coming to a close, think how much the Father loves *Creation*. If you feel you have no influence, think again when aligning with the depth of the Father's love. Our world cannot wait much longer!

Throughout this work, I wrote much about God's intention. Jesus gave us the prayer about the Father's "...will be done on earth as it is in heaven." And we have attached the Father's will to deliver us from sin and temptation. Unfortunately, it's a beautiful prayer, but the vision of our ancestors circumvented the intended meaning.

When Jesus read in the Synagogue, he chose a passage to unveil a dream beyond all men and women's imaginations about God's love and intentions for humanity. And he does not just leave it at that. Instead, he added, "...in your hearing, this Scripture is fulfilled." He declared a new paradigm, yet we return to the old-world view of sin and punishment. That is not the fullness of prayer Jesus gave to us.

So, I ask you, Jesus, how do we reconcile the discrepancy between the new paradigm rooted in God's favor and then returning to an old ground leaning on sin and God's disapproval?

> You do not have to compose a new prayer in my name
> to reconcile. Only to know the truth of the Father's
> intention to embrace and heal the human family. And as
> you lament, this is less the case, and more the problem
> I came to remedy.

Interestingly, in some form, many still weigh in on the Father's wrath. Yet, who has witnessed the wrath of God? On the other hand, I hear numbers of people talk about God's blessings! Nevertheless, God's wrath in biblical history is daunting. And how much of biblical history mistakes the undoing of humanity for the work of God?

I know when I do not like what I see, sometimes, I wish to push back, but that is not God's way! God has only one way. We do a great job of rejecting one another, sometimes just by the way a person may look. Countless remarks sling left and right every day. How many people sitting on a park bench are watching, laughing, criticizing, or judging others?

If you came across God sitting on a park bench, he would not be criticizing or judging you. That is why God would say illnesses multiply, and we are the cause through the words we utter. God would look at each one and see in them the marvel that each one is, in and of themselves. Such is the Father's love and loving intent for humankind. The Father neither thrives nor does he draw on negative energy. Such was never the way of the Son.

Returning to the "power of intention," many have discovered a powerful field from which to manifest our intentions. Indeed, before we are born, God's intentions are already with us and waiting for us to fulfill (Jer 1:5). That does not mean we are without choices. Instead, our choices are numerous. However, as we align in accord with God's intent, the soul is satisfied, and our direction affirmed.

God is not judging our choices but always communicating. If we are listening and attentive, the more we experience why we are here and what we are to do. The soul's direction is not to rush or to press on us. My life testifies to that, and the journey is worth every breath along the way.

When asking the Father what we are to build and how are we to unfold our purpose, he responds,

> Turn to the place of your heart and, when seeing that I am there, ask, Father what do you wish me to do in your name? If I hear the beat of your heart, you will know what to do. If not, come back repeatedly until you know.

For some, God's response may sound elusive, but I tell you the Father is not, though often speaking in metaphors. Here, I offer a story of my own that conveys an avenue for understanding how God may be in communication with you. In it, the stage is set for a lifelong adventure to begin.

Like many seekers, I pose questions to God to find my way through life and purpose. At times, it meant getting a good job, and God would provide. As I got older, I wanted something more. I did not feel I was fulfilling my purpose, not the one that I felt I was meant to fulfill.

One day, I got into my boat, thinking of creating an open space somewhere in the middle of Narragansett Bay. I thought to be loud in voice, yet in a private setting and sure to get God's attention! I was thirsty for an answer and frustrated, not knowing my role in life. Burning inside me, I held onto the question of direction that would satisfy the meaning I so desired. When I reached a point in the middle of the bay, I dropped the anchor. I was so anxious to begin, I foolishly forgot the anchor would never reach the bottom.

Nevertheless, it made me fully aware of the vulnerable space I created.

I shut the motor off and sat for a pause to ponder why I was there. Then, I finally stood up, lifted my fist to the sky, and raised my voice to God, "What do you want me to do with my life?" I looked up, and the sun was beginning to fade in the momentum of gray clouds. Still, I thought I might hear God's booming voice but heard only the sound of shuffling waves. In what seemed like only a moment, the clouds darkened, and they quickly rolled forward. The storm was building, and in a moment of fright, I reached for the anchor. I could not pull it up fast enough, and then the rain started to come down and the clouds were getting thicker and the waves more intense.

To my dismay, the storm also came with a most extraordinary experience. Amid the squall, I drifted into an occasion of rapture. Peacefully, voyaging back to the docks, I sensed God was speaking to me! Rain was pouring all around me, and the waves were lifting, yet I never experienced a more tranquil moment. I did not hear any words, but in the experience, I knew God heard me! I will never forget the most beautiful moment in the middle of a storm. It did not end my quest, but it was only the beginning or knowing that God is with me. He is listening, and my heart is aligning with his.

When looking back, I see that I still needed time. Asking God questions is easy but trusting that you are where God wants you to be in every moment is the greater task. Believe that as your heart stays close, he will lead you to your soul's desire. That is God's intention imbued within the depths of each soul. And now, as never before, God desires to draw you close.

However, be mindful that wherever God may take you is not necessarily the direction you may expect or anticipate. But when acknowledging God is with you in every moment, that is your compass to journey safely into your soul's desire. No one can tell you the course, but that is not to deny there are some who can guide you. That is the gift of a good spiritual counselor or director.

Engaging God is between you, God, and your soul's desire even before birth. The prophet Jeremiah attests to God's plan for him, and it does not begin and end with him:

> Before I formed you in the womb I knew you,
> and before you were born I consecrated you;
> I appointed you a prophet to the nations (Jer 1:5).

A Call to Love

The Temple that Jesus Built

A serene landscape opens before me. Beneath the soft blue sky, the sun's golden rays are blazing through the cotton-like clouds. Through them, two mighty hands elevate the Eucharist more radiant than the sun. The Father's promise swells within and shrouds me with joy, and the Father's voice reveals:

I say this is a magnificent image, a glorified image that promises holiness in concert with God. Indeed, it does, but not everything is as it seems. To be in harmony with me is not about venerating a symbol or action within a single moment. Honoring me is about embodying me in your every step. And with each day, you become me. And you ask, 'How is this possible? The way is beyond human to be as one with you?' And I tell you that is not so, and the rules are simple.

I left you the pretext for the Church set upon the foundation of my love. The call is service to one another. I do not say the kingdom comes without questions and answers along the way, but that you have a solid foundation on which to build. Did not Jesus say houses raised on weak foundations will fall? Well, foundations are falling. And did not my Son say he would raise the Temple in three days? Upon what is written within this text's pages, my Temple can rise in a single day!

I hand you the foundation of my Son: No laws, rules, and precepts, but to be in service to one another. The idea speaks for itself that you respect all creation and all things when in service to one another.

It follows then to manage your resources and distribute them for the good of all. Humankind has moved forward very quickly and is at a threshold now. The earth is falling because you are falling in your service. The scope is sweeping, and your fate teeters or stabilizes according to your decisions. Big decisions are before you, and they can be made wisely for the good of all. The question is: Will you make them?

Many officials will say that Jesus left no blueprint for building the Church. Many believe the apostles were of little faith, and perhaps, that's why Paul's work overshadowed theirs. However, one is misled to think that the apostles failed or that Jesus was unsuccessful in gathering adequate followers. No! He and the apostles did not fail at all.

They did not need to write down every word about what it means to love. To do so is to constrain the definition of God. If we have nothing else from Jesus, what is left is the imprint that he loved and with love so extraordinary and vibrant that many died by his side. Here is the blueprint from which to build, and perhaps, the central point of contention between the apostles and Paul. And clearly, the enemy is fear.

Jesus did not empower his followers with laws and rules to guide the way. Instead, he taught them to trust in the Father's love.

He said to the Pharisees, "You blind guides with all your laws and rules you weigh people down." Jesus did not choose the learned men who would create more problems for him. Jesus etches into his followers' hearts the love of God, which is the one blueprint on which to build. What is the more solid ground? What better compass than to align oneself with the Father's heart and therein *Love's* realm. Undoubtedly, the responsibility is placed in our hands to align with God's heart. We are not fallen, especially when standing together with love enough to change the world.

Father, is it too simple to summarize that your call is "to love," and so also, the life and death of your Son founded on the same calling? Then, why do innumerable churches tip the scales with the weight of sin and repentance instead of Jesus' call to love?

> Although people are tied up in knots over this, the answer is simple. The ideology of men restrains my love. The messages within these pages are gifts of the Son for resurrecting my truth!

Instead of carrying crosses for sin and retribution, our highest call is to carry the Father's heart. We cannot pay God back but only to freely love God, who loves beyond our wildest dreams. And then, we are to share God's love within the boundaries of our world. I am grateful for God's work in me and for those who have ears to hear. I genuinely know what we mean to the Father and the creation God places in our hands. My cup overflows to realize the depths by which God loves men, women, and children; and no less for a magnified view of "All that is." My wish for all who read is that your cup spills over. Yet, more significantly, this is the Father's desire before mine.

I used to preach to my congregation that God needs you. I was not sure why exactly, but I felt it in my heart. Now, I know why and if I did my job, now, you know too! Although I am shaped by a Catholic upbringing that I will always treasure, my roots are from God as with all people. So too, the call is for all "who have ears to hear and eyes to see" the *Love* that shapes us and calls us to a higher paradigm.

Jesus, do you have a final word?

If I were to stand before all who read the pages of this book, I would say, blessed are you whose heart opens to my truth.

Eloquently expressed through a song written by Nat King Cole and released on March 29, 1948, he drafts a breathtaking image of the Father's intention from the beginning, unbeknown to the artist. The hit title was "Nature Boy" about a young man who traveled the world to discover that the most meaningful thing in life is to love and receive love. Capturing the incredibly profound image of God's intention for humanity, the lyric is God's first before all others. Speaking to the prophet Jeremiah, God put it this way two thousand six hundred years ago: "And you shall be my people, and I will be your God" (Jer 30:22).

Jesus foreshadows that we will do "...greater things than he" (Jn 14:12). He shows us the Father, who loves us first and teaches us to love in return. He gives his life, teaching us how! On that ground, we can do extraordinary things. That is because we are the builders of God's kingdom. We are the vessels of the Father's life, and to love is how Jesus taught us to live because that is who the Father is and the image in which we are made. Central to his final words to his followers, Jesus said:

As the Father has loved me, so I have loved you; abide in my love. If you keep my commandments, you will abide in my love, just as I have kept my Father's commandments and abide in his love. I have said these things to you so that my joy may be in you, and that your joy may be complete.

The Father intends for us to become the vessels of his love for the life and transformation of the world, and here are the greater things that Jesus says we will do (Jn 14:12). He taught us the way not only in his life but with his blood and the blood of his dearest followers who saw no other way!

Return to the Wheatfield

In the beginning, when opening the corridor into God's kingdom, I received the vision of the "Wheatfield," and Jesus places the Eucharist in my hands. Again, the Father reveals the *Bread* held high in his hands. So, I ask why? Am I once again called to celebrate the Eucharist?

What is more meaningful, my messenger, to eat the Eucharist or become the love that gives the Holy Communion? Of course, the answer is to become the love, which is the message of the Eucharist I offer. And the message of this book I give through you. This book is Holy Communion, not bread to eat but the love of God to digest!

Selected References

Arnold, Duane W.H and Robert Hudson Beyond belief: *What the Martyrs said to God*, Zondervan, Grand Rapids, Michigan, 2002.

Augustine, St. City of God: *Concerning the City of God against Pagan*, Translated by Henry Bettenson, London, England, Penguin Books 1972.

Barclay, William: *The Acts of the Apostles*, Revised Edition, The Westminster Press, Philadelphia, 1976.

Barclay, William: *The Letters to the Corinthians*, Revised Edition, The Westminster Press, Philadelphia, 1975.

Bokenkotter, Thomas: *A Concise History of the Catholic Church*, Revised Edition, Image Books: Doubleday, New York, NY, 1990.

Boucher, Madeline I. The Parables: *New Testament Message*, Vol.7, Revised Edition, Michael Glazier, Inc. Wilmington, Delaware, 1983.

Bring, Ragnar: *Commentary of Galatians*, Translated by Eric Wahlstrom, Mulhenberg Press, Philadelphia, 1961.

Brown, Harold O.J. Heresies: *Heresy and Orthodoxy in the History of the Church*, Hendrickson Publishers, Inc, Peabody, Massachusetts, 1988.

Comby, Jean: *How to read Church History*, Vol.1 From the Beginnings to the Fifteenth Century, Translated by John Bowden and Margaret Lydamore from the French Pour lire L' Histoire de L'Eglise Tome 1, 1984 by Les Editions du Cerf 29 bd Latour-Mabourg, Paris, Crossroad Publishing Co., New York, NY, 1985.

Comby, Jean and Diarmaid MacCulloch: *How to read Church History*, Vol. 2, From the Reformation to the Present Day, Translated by Margaret Lydamore and John Bowden from the French Pour lire l' Histoire de l' Eglise Tome 2, 1986 by Les Editions du Cerf 29 bd Latour-Mabourg, Paris, 1986, Crossroad Publishing Co., New York, NY, 2000.

Comfort, Philip W, and Wendell C. Hawley: *Opening the Gospel of John*, Tyndale House Publishers, Inc. Wheaton, Illinois, 1994.

Crowe, Jerome, C.P. The Acts: *New Testament Message*, Vol. 8, Michael Glazier, Inc. Wilmington, Delaware, 1979.

Eisenbaum, Pamela Paul was not a Christian: The Original Message of a Misunderstood Apostle, Harper Collins Publishers, New York, NY, 2009.

Fallon, Francis T. 2 Corinthians: *New Testament Message*, Vol. 11, Michael Glazier, Inc., Wilmington, Delaware, 1980.

Francis, St. of Assisi Writings and Early Biographies, English Omnibus of the Sources for the Life of St. Francis, Fourth Revised

Edition, Edited by Marion A. Habig, Translations by Raphael Brown, Benen Fahy, Placid Hermann, Paul Oligny, Nesta de Robeck, Leo Sherley-Price, Franciscan Press, Quincy University, Quincy, Illinois, 1991.

Fryne, Sean: *The World of the New Testament: New Testament Message*, Vol. 2, Michael Glazier, Inc., Wilmington, Delaware, 1989.

Harrington, S.J., Daniel J. Interpreting the New Testament: A Practical Guide, The Liturgical Press, Collegeville, Minnesota, 1979.

Harrington, S.J., Daniel J.: *Interpreting the Old Testament: A Practical Guide*, The Liturgical Press, Collegeville, Minnesota, 1981.

Heidegger, Martin: *Being and Time*, Translated from the German Sein und Zeit Seventh Edition, Neomarius Verlag, Tubingen by John Macquarrie and Edward Robinson, New York, NY, Harper & Row Publishing, 1962.

Hobbes, Thomas: *Leviathan*, Penguin Random House, UK, 1651.

Huck-Lietzmann Gospel Parallels: *A Synopsis of the First Three Gospels*, Ninth Edition, 1936, Edited by Burton H. Throckmorton, Jr., Fourth Edition Revised, Thomas Nelson Publishers, Nashville, TN, 1979.

Kamen, Henry: *The Spanish Inquisition: A Historical Revision*, Fourth Edition, Yale University Press, New Haven & London, 2014.

Liderbach, Daniel: *Christ in the Early Christian Hymns*, Paulist Press, Mahwah, NJ, 1998.

Maher M.S.C, Michael: *Genesis, Old Testament 2*, Edited by Carol Stuhlmueller, C.P. and Martin McNamara, Michael Glazier, Inc., Wilmington, Delaware, 1982.

McGrath, Alister: *A History of Defending the Truth*, Harper One Publishers, New York, NY, 2009.

Newsome Jr., James D.: *The Hebrew Prophets*, John Know Press, Atlanta, Georgia, 1984.

Osiek, Carolyn, R.S.C.J Galatians: New Testament Message 12, Michael Glazier, Inc. Edited by Wilfrid Harrington, O.P. and Donald Senior, C.P., Wilmington, Delaware, 1980.

The Navarre Bible Acts of the Apostles, translated by Michael Adams ,1989, Edited by James Gavigan, Brian McCarthy, Thomas McGovern, Four Courts Press, Dublin, Ireland, 1992.

Turner, Denys Thomas Aquinas: *A Portrait*, Yale University Press, New Haven, 2013.

Van de Weyer, Robert: *The Harper Collins Book of Prayers: A treasury of Prayers*, A Treasury of Prayers Through the Age, Harper San Francisco, A Division of Harper Collins, 1993.

Wylie, J.A.: *The History of the Waldenses*, Cassell and Company 1860, copyright 2016.

About the Author

At age 34, in September of 1987, Rev. Douglas Simon Sweet entered St. John's Seminary College, Boston, MA, to earn a Bachelor of Philosophy degree. By June 1994, he received a Bachelor of Sacred Theology and a Master of Divinity at St. Mary's Seminary & University, Baltimore, MD. In June 1995, he was ordained a Catholic priest at the Cathedral of Saints Peter and Paul, Providence, RI.

After ten years, the intensity of his call diminished. However, the setback opened yet another doorway into his calling. By June 2016, he received a vision, and the inspiration continued for years.

Learning of God's desire to reconcile the fears standing between God and God's people weighed heavily on Rev. Sweet. As though he were carrying the weight of God's sorrow, he had to know where and how the erosion of humanity's relationship with God began. The quest led him to unveil lifegiving revelations of the Father and the Son buried in a dark history.

Over 2500 years ago, God's heart was revealed to the prophet Jeremiah when saying to him, "I will be your God, and you will be my people." How many have forgotten or even believed in God's desire? Rev. Sweet avows, "I never thought such words from God would sound again in today's world, and certainly not through me."

To reach Rev. Douglas Simon Sweet directly, please write to him at:
RevDouglasSimon@mail.com
RevDouglasSimonSweet.com

www.ingramcontent.com/pod-product-compliance
Lightning Source LLC
Chambersburg PA
CBHW050321160726
48002CB00001B/125